Why Wages Rise

F. A. HARPER

THE FOUNDATION FOR ECONOMIC EDUCATION, INC.

IRVINGTON-ON-HUDSON, NEW YORK   1957

Published by the Foundation for Economic Education, FEE.org.

Large Print Edition published 2012 by Skyler J. Collins.
Visit: www.skylerjcollins.com

Cover image by StockFreeImages.com.

ISBN-13: 978-1480031272
ISBN-10: 1480031275

Contents

Charts and Tables

Introduction

WAGES are of prime importance in any advanced economy such as ours. They affect us all far more than seems evidenced in our concern about them.

Everyone buys wages, in a sense, with every purchase he makes. And three-fourths of all incomes in the United States represent pay for work done in the employ of another. So nearly every one of us is on both sides of the wage exchange, in one way or another.

We all know in a general way that wages have been rising for a long time in this country, but there is evidence aplenty that the economic principles which apply to wage problems are not well understood. Probably they are no better understood now than in the early thirties when measures adopted to combat the depression proved to be such colossal failures. Fearing another depression like that which followed World War I, we now seem enmeshed in chronic and progressive inflation, which Lenin once said was a sure and simple way to destroy the capitalist system. Our "prosperity" now seems to be riding on the horns of a dilemma that will surely end in the destruction of capitalism unless we can resolve this problem which in large measure is a wage problem.

I shall deal with the wage problem in a manner that may seem oversimplified. Basic principles always have a way of seeming simple. Yet if they be principles, they can no more be oversimplified than can the law of gravity or the listing of chemical elements be oversimplified. What is needed in our complex society of millions of products sold by millions of business units to over a hundred million traders through billions of transactions each year is to get back to simple economic principles. These are working tools for solving problems that seem more complex than they really are.

Two Roadblocks

In helping another person to resolve this wage problem, it seems to me that two roadblocks to his understanding may first have to be removed. They obstruct a thorough insight into the wage problem.

One roadblock is the difference between money wages and real wages, which results in serious misconceptions. In a period of inflation such as we have long been enduring, or of deflation, a comparison of money wages in two separate years tells you no more about their relative worth than would a comparison of a daily wage in the United States with that of Chile — $10 as compared with 5,000 pesos, for instance. Money wages must first be converted into real wages before we can see their patterns of change.

The other roadblock has to do with the effect of unions on wages. If you were to describe an elephant to a person who has never seen one and who had never even seen a picture of one, you probably would not describe a flea and then say that an elephant doesn't look like that. This would not be very helpful unless the person believed that an elephant looked like a flea. In the case of unions, there seems to be a firm and widespread belief about their effect on wages such that this question must be dealt with at the outset. So we shall start there.

When speaking of wages and what makes them rise, the meaning will be the over-all level of wages — the general welfare, in that sense. To speak otherwise of wages, such as wage rates for one or a few persons, would involve special situations which are not the object of this discussion. A bank robber might succeed in gaining a high wage for his hour of work; a few persons, through power and special privilege, might likewise gain some short-time advantages at the expense of the others who work. But such gains of some wage earners at the expense of other wage earners are not the aim or meaning of this analysis of why wages rise.

1. Labor Unions

Wage rates are higher in the United States than in any other country. And they are about five times as high here as they were a century ago, in purchasing power.

The recent joining of the two major labor unions in the United States met with mixed emotions. On the one hand, such concentration of power anywhere in society frightens those who know its evil consequences. But on the other hand, the move is accepted as part of the long-time progress of unionization which is commonly believed to be the cause of our high and rising wages. "So," say many, "the fruits are worth the risk."

Superficial Observation

The belief that unions cause wages to rise seems to be borne out by simple observation: In repeated instances it is observed that a labor union demands a rise in wages for its members. An argument ensues between the union and management; there may even be a strike. Sooner or later a wage rise is granted — if not for the full amount requested, at least for a major part of it. Other firms then have to meet this new rate or lose workers. So it appears, ipso facto, that wages in general are raised by union activity.

Such a close-up observation, however, may lead one to see things that are not so, as the proverbial fly on the chariot wheel believed that it propelled the vehicle. One must stand off a bit from the publicized union activities if he is to gain a true perspective on whether they cause average wage rates to rise. One needs, for this purpose, a telescopic view by which to compare the long-time trends of wage rates with changes in union membership.

The Past Century

On the accompanying chart, hourly wage rates in the United States are shown by the upper line. Wages will now buy nearly five times what they would a hundred years ago. The chart is constructed so that a constant *rate* of change in real wages would appear as a sloping straight line. Progress in an advancing economy seems to work that way, so that wages tend to rise in the manner of compound interest.

Wage trends in the United States over the past century have fallen into three distinct periods: a yearly increase of 1.27 per cent for the period 1855-1895, a yearly increase of 0.55 per cent for 1896-1916, and a yearly increase of 2.47 per cent for 1917-1955. The reason for these changes in trend is a large question, which will be considered here only as it relates to union membership.

The lower line on the chart shows union membership in per cent of all "gainful workers" in the United States. Here too are three distinct levels: A negligible union membership prior to 1900, then a rise at the turn of the century to a level of about 6 to 9 per cent which prevailed from 1903 to 1936, and then a sharp rise to a little over one-fourth of all workers as members of unions for the past ten years.

So the trend in wage rates and in the proportion of work-

WAGES AND UNION MEMBERSHIP — UNITED STATES

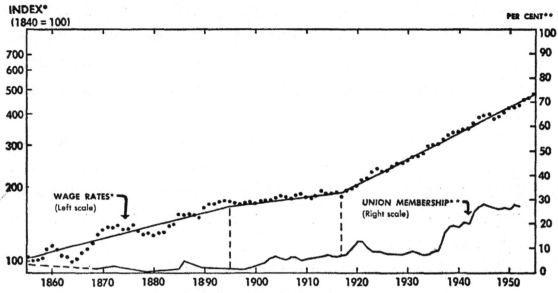

INDEX* (1840 = 100)

PER CENT**

WAGE RATES* (Left scale)

UNION MEMBERSHIP** (Right scale)

*Wage rates are in terms of what could be bought with an hour's wage.
**Union membership is in per cent of all gainful workers.

SOURCE: The Tucker series, converted to hourly rates and adjusted to cost of living, *Employment and Wages in the United States* by W. S. Woytinsky and Associates (New York: The Twentieth Century Fund, 1953), pages 582-583 for years 1855 to 1890; from 1891 to 1955, linked series from same source, page 586, with hourly wage rates adjusted by consumer's price index, page 176; and *Economic Report of the President,* January 1955, page 162; and *Survey of Current Business,* United States Department of Commerce.

Membership of Unions from *Employment and Wages in the United States* by W. S. Woytinsky and Associates (New York: The Twentieth Century Fund, 1953), pages 233, 234, and 642; *Statistical Abstract,* 1955, page 219; *Historical Statistics of the United States, 1789-1945,* page 72.

Gainfully employed workers, from *Historical Statistics of the United States, 1789-1945,* pages 64 and 65 (interpolated from census years' data for 1855 figure); *Statistical Abstract,* 1955, page 187. See also *Economic Almanac, 1953-1954,* National Industrial Conference Board, pages 418-419.

ers who are union members have each had three distinctive periods during the past century. But if we compare the two lines carefully, no noticeable relationship between the two is to be found. Neither wage rates nor union membership could be predicted from the other, with any accuracy what-

11

soever. Try it. After covering the lower line, try to draw one to represent union membership based only on this evidence about wage trends, and vice versa. By comparing your estimate with the facts, I'm sure you will agree that changes in wage rates are quite unrelated to changes in union membership.

1. *Assumption:* If unions were presumed to be the cause of rising wages, one would expect wages to have been at their lowest point — and to have remained at about the same low point — from 1855 to about 1900, when union membership was negligible.

Fact: Wages rose appreciably over the period. They doubled within a man's working lifetime.

2. *Assumption:* Whatever the cause of the rising wage rates in the earlier period when union membership was negligible, one would expect it to have continued. But he would, in addition, expect the rise to be accelerated with the rise in union membership about the turn of the century.

Fact: The rate of rise in wage rates from 1896 to 1916 was less than half that of the previous fifty years.

3. *Assumption:* One would expect the sharpest rise in wage rates to come when union membership was having its most rapid increase — from 1936 to 1945 — and then to have leveled off when union membership stopped rising.

Fact: The rate of increase in wage rates which began at the close of World War I continued with amazing consistency for the entire period from 1917 to 1955.

From this evidence one must conclude, I believe, that wage rates show no clear response whatever to changes in union membership.

If one says that the two lines are related but there is a lag in time of some 15 to 20 years, the evidence would be that rising wage rates cause union membership to rise, not vice versa. In any event it is the opposite of the theory that unions cause wage rates to rise. Consequences do not happen before their causes.

And so this popular illusion that rising wages are due to the growth of labor unions must be discarded if there is to be any room for attention to other possible causes.

As a preview to the answer as to what makes wages rise, I will merely say here that wages can be paid only out of what is produced. Something other than your joining a union is what increases your hourly economic output — now five times that of your great-grandfather's a century ago.

2. Productivity

An employee of General Motors is likely to wonder at times why his pay can't be raised. "Even if it were doubled or trebled," he may complain to his wife, "it would never be felt by GM."

True enough. During 1955 the average pay of an employee of GM was $5,011. Yet GM's profits for the year were $1,189,477,082 (or $3,751,477,082 before any ascertainable taxes) on a total business of $12,443,277,420. It can be seen at a glance that doubling the pay of this employee would be no more noticeable in the whole enterprise than would be the adding of another automobile to those now owned in the State of Michigan.

Doubling the pay of all GM employees, however, would be quite a different story. It would eat up *in one year* more than the total value of the firm's real estate, plants, and equipment.

I am not concerned here with GM's wage problem as such. I do not know whether their present wage scale is too low, too high, or just right. The only present purpose of these figures is to illustrate the difference between a narrow view and a broad view of the wage problem.

An automobile is the sum of many simple parts working together in simple ways. In like manner a complex economic problem is composed of simple elements which can best be seen by looking under the hood, so to speak.

In trying to see what makes wages rise, let's consider first a lone pioneer instead of a single employee of GM. He is producing things entirely for his own use. What he produces — potatoes, etc. — is his wage. He needs no Ph.D. in economics to know that he can consume only what he has produced, and no more. The only way he could double his wage would be to produce twice as much. He couldn't raise his wage by as much as one per cent except by producing more. This is like saying that $1 = 1$.

Now if a neighbor moves in, the two pioneers might trade with each other some of what each produces — let us say in equal amounts. The same rule would still hold true. Together they could consume only what they have produced. Or we might say that $1 + 1 = 2$.

As the society increases, eventually reaching a laboring force of 63 million, the same would still be true.

Not all persons in a nation's economy, of course, produce the same things. Nor do they produce the same amounts. Furthermore, some work alone and others work in groups as in a corporation. It has been estimated, for instance, that there are nine million different business enterprises or farms in the United States, and some eight million different commodity items or services in which they deal.

Production Comes First

Estimates have even been attempted of the total amount of production for all these producers, added together in terms of dollars of presumed worth. For 1955 the total estimated figure was $322 billion. Goods and services were added together, roughly, on the basis of consumers' appraisals of their

CHANGES IN PRODUCTIVITY AND WAGE RATES — UNITED STATES

PER CENT OF AVERAGE (Ratio scale)

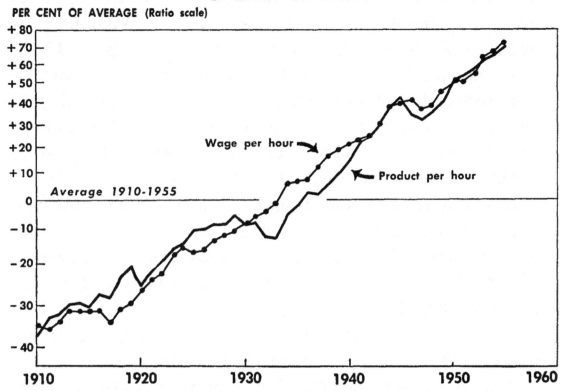

SOURCE: This chart is designed so that a constant percentage increase would appear as a straight line. The values of product and wages are both expressed in dollars of constant buying power. The data for product are for the private sector, and are from the series by John W. Kendrick in his paper, *National Productivity and Its Long-Term Projection* (National Bureau of Economic Research, May 1951), brought up to date by the National Industrial Conference Board. For the data on wage rates, see Chapter 1, p. 11.

worth in relation to one another. I can't vouch for the accuracy of any such total figure. In fact, the task seems impossible for more than one reason. But even so, this much can be said about it: Whatever the right figure may have been, the only way to have doubled it as such (in stable dollars) would have been to have produced twice as much. There is no way by which arbitrary action or edict could have raised it by as much as one per cent, unless it had somehow increased production.

No more need be said about productivity and its importance in the question of what makes wages rise. The simple principle involved, for one person or for 63 million persons in an exchange economy, is that consumption cannot be more than production.

Wages Parallel Productivity

Some want to know, however, whether the facts on wage rates square with this theory. Has the history of the United States borne this out?

Some estimates of the value of output per hour for the private sector of the national economy have been made available, giving us a basis for comparing productivity with wage rates since 1910 (see chart). The relationship is close, except in a few instances.

From 1930 to 1933 real wages ran considerably ahead of productivity — or more accurately, wages continued their upward trend despite falling productivity. But a readjustment soon got under way, and the seemingly excess wage rate was completely corrected by 1941. On the other hand, wages seemed to fail to share fully the increases in productivity from 1916 to 1919, and again in the middle twenties.

If our theory is sound, one may wonder why any divergence at all between the two occurred. One reason might be errors in the data, of course. Another is that the two are not precisely different expressions of the same thing, as are "production" and "product wage" for a lone pioneer. Not all our national product goes for wage payments. Roughly, about two-thirds of it goes for wages and salaries, with the remainder divided about equally between (1) pay for current effort by those who are self-employed, and (2) payment for the use of savings that have been invested in tools and equipment.

But the matter of dividing available goods and services into pay for current work as distinguished from pay for savings from past work is another subject, to be discussed subsequently. Present concern is with the relationship between wages and productivity. The correspondence is close, as it must be, because wages must come from production and can rise on a sustained basis only from increased productivity.

3. Dividing The Pie

Higher wages come from increased output per hour of work. This is not a new or profound discovery. For how could consumption be greater than production?

Wages, however, are not the only part of the economic pie. Why, then, couldn't wages be raised by giving the employee a larger share?

For purposes of this discussion, the pie of personal incomes may be thought of as divided into two parts. One is the pay for work done currently and the other is pay for the use of savings — income from work done in the past and not used for consumption at that time.

Pay for work done currently includes wages and salaries, or the equivalent in some other form of economic reward. On the other hand, income from the use of savings includes interest on money loaned, dividends on shares of ownership, rent on real estate, and the like.

A person who has never saved a cent and who owns no tools of his own may be getting all his income from work done currently, using tools that have been provided by the savings of others. Another person — perhaps an aged person — may be idle so far as current economic effort is concerned, getting all his income as pay for the use of his past savings. More commonly, a person receives part of his income from each of these sources, getting some from current effort and some from savings.

Some persons work for themselves, using in full or in part tools provided from their own savings. And some persons work for others.

There are all sorts of combinations of income from these two sources. But in some form or degree, essentially everyone in the United States has savings or property and is therefore a capitalist. Most persons also have some income from work done currently.

Present Divisions of the Pie

Information about the present division of the economic pie can be found in figures supplied by the Department of Commerce.[1]

The average personal income in the United States was about $4,600 in 1955. Of this amount, something like 85 per cent, or $3,910, appears to have been pay for work done currently. The remaining 15 per cent, or about $690, was pay to savers who were providing the tools of production in one form or another.

Were the entire pie to go to wage earners and others as pay for current work — as advocated by Karl Marx, to be explained shortly — wages could go up from 85 to 100, or about one-sixth. And even this much rise could occur only if there were no reduction in the size of the total pie — that is, in total production.

But let's assume that no decline were to occur in total production. How important, then, would be the rise in wages

---

[1]*Survey of Current Business*, National Income Number, July 1955, and corresponding issues in earlier years. United States Department of Commerce.

20

compared with the rise caused by increased productivity which was discussed in the two previous chapters? Since 1917, wage rates have risen with increased productivity at about 2.5 per cent a year. Thus in six years' time this rise in wages would equal the 15 per cent increase possible from getting all the remainder of the pie. Or to put it another way, productivity increases during the past working generation have raised wages perhaps six times as much as could possibly come from diverting to wages every cent of current returns for savings.

Wages can, furthermore, continue to rise indefinitely so long as productivity continues to increase. But a gain in wages from a larger share of the pie is a gain which can be repeated only once. Any increase from that source can go only from the 85 to 100 per cent, and no further. A dead end to improvement is then reached, because a pie of more than 100 per cent is not possible.

Adverse Effects on Savings

Capital created from savings makes possible a large part of our production. It apparently raises the average income in the United States to a level of $4,600 instead of perhaps $200 to $250 — as it would be if there were essentially no tools. This teamwork between those who save and those who use the tools is the reason for our high and rising wage rates. Without a continuous and increasing supply of tools, the gear wheels of economic progress would be slowed or even stopped.

Without a return for savings, where would future tools come from to enhance the fruits of current effort? Who would then be willing to save and invest in tools, if obliged to take all the risk without any prospect of return? Few persons would save till tomorrow what they could consume today, unless they were rewarded for doing so.

During the last quarter-century inroads have been made into the reward for savings, with serious consequences. The rate at which personal savings are being invested in productive tools, as compared with earlier decades, has declined. Among what we call "savings" are government bonds, which in reality are investments in a deficit of the government — not a productive tool any more than would be your tax receipt. And some of what is called "savings" has been forced upon individuals, in a sense, as a direct or indirect consequence of present tax policies.

Over the last quarter-century the costs of government have nearly trebled in proportion to personal incomes, going up from 12 to 34 per cent. It is impossible, of course, to know for certain how heavily this has been a burden on pay for savings as compared to pay for current work. But there have been large increases in the graduated taxes on both individual incomes and corporate incomes — the "double tax" — and the government has held down interest rates in order to help the sale of its (deficit) bonds. This has unquestionably reduced the share of the pie going as pay for real savings.

History of an Idea

An increased share of the pie going to wages, at the expense of the share for savings, is not just an accident. It is the wayward son of a notorious ideological ancestor. Its pedigree needs critical study by those of us who have faith in a system of personal responsibility and freedom of opportunity in economic affairs. Plausible on the surface, this idea has seduced many who today denounce it by name but embrace its substance.

During most of his ten million or more years of history, man has presumably been his own employer, producing most of his own food, raiment, and shelter — though, of course, we do not know the unknown. But if it is true that in most instances he worked for himself, or perhaps joined other huntsmen and producers in informal cooperation, such a type of livelihood would hardly have permitted him to embrace the notion that one's welfare can be improved by claiming a larger share of his own pie. No sane person is going to demand more wage from himself for his muscular work, at the expense of his management self or his tool-owning self.

Slavery Was Tried

Somewhere along man's historic trail some men began to enslave others to work for them. Slaves doubtless wanted a larger share of what was produced, but there wasn't much they could do about it because the master held full ownership of the slave. And anyhow, in those early slave-holding days each person was able to produce little more than enough to keep himself from starving, and so a master couldn't take much of what a slave produced or he would have a slave no more.

In more recent times the voluntary employer-employee arrangement among free men has largely displaced slavery throughout the world. Some work for others at a wage. They may want to do so as a way of gaining the use of tools with which to work, or because for some other reason the wage offered is more enticing than the rewards in prospect while working for themselves.

By this arrangement, persons sell in the market what they have jointly produced. And when this is done, the problem of dividing the pie arises in a new form. Instead of a slave who can do nothing about it except bemoan his plight as he wearily hoes his row, the employee can — if he so desires — go elsewhere to seek an easier livelihood or higher pay.

Labor and Surplus Value Theories

From this new economic climate there arose, in the course of time, the *labor theory of value* which has become highly appealing to some among the employee class. It is often used in one way or another in bargaining for wages, which are now a form of price and therefore the object of higgling and haggling in the market, as is the price of wheat or potatoes.

On its surface the labor theory of value seems plausible enough. Suppose you are a self-employed person and consume what you produce. If you have to work twice as long to produce one thing you want as to produce another, it would seem that you must prize the former twice as much as the latter. If this were not so, wouldn't you have produced something else instead? Something requiring three times the labor must be prized three times as much, etc. In like manner, the labor theory of value assumes that labor is the essential ingredient by which to measure all value.

The labor theory of value had just nicely gained some respectable acceptance among economists of that early day when along came a man — Karl Marx — with a cause which fitted this theory tragically well. Others before Marx had, of course, held essentially the same views about value. But Marx set in motion forces which have brought the world to the brink of disaster in economic, social, and political affairs.

Having accepted the labor theory of value from the classical economists, Marx a century ago attempted to explain how profit to private owners worms its wily way into exchange by way of the capitalist system. All return on capital, according to Marx, comes out of the value that labor has created and is just another form of theft that capitalism has tried to make respectable. This concept of profits is a logical descendant of the labor theory of value.

No Return on Capital

Marx viewed a return on capital in the same manner as a doctor views a parasite feasting on his patient. For if all value comes from labor and is in proportion thereto, any share of the pie going to anyone other than the laborer, in proportion to his labor, must be the result of a parasitical attachment by capitalists.

The devilment in the capitalist setup, according to Marx, is made possible by the private ownership of the land, materials, and tools with which labor does its work. The capitalist owner who holds title to these material means of production can, in this way, claim ownership of the product. He can then withhold any part of it he wishes from the laborer — the one who Marx claimed was the rightful owner of all of it because he is the one who created all its value in the first place.

So pay for the use of capital is like loot from theft, as

Marx saw it. He said that the absolute amount of profit is equal to the absolute amount of *surplus value*. Persons who hold these Marxian beliefs charge that the laboring man is "exploited" by the capitalist owner; that he is a "wage-slave" of the capitalist.

The term surplus value was defined by Marx, then, as the part of production which, under private ownership, is confiscated by the capitalist from its rightful owner, the laborer. That is the part which all Marxians believe can and should be reclaimed by labor. The amount of surplus value, by this concept, measures the amount that wages could rise aside from any increase in hourly output. Were labor to regain this lost part of the economic pie, it would simply mean taking it back from the capitalist thief.

Tools Make the Difference

Some ten million years ago man's tools probably were simple ones, like a stone fastened to the end of a stick. We may assume incomes then were essentially all reward for current work, rather than being a reward for savings from past effort stored in the form of tools to aid in production. The labor theory of value may seem to have applied fairly well then because essentially all production was the result of direct and current labor. True or false, the surplus value theory could hardly have been of concern then, and putting it into practice could have done little damage to their meager living.

But today, being as dependent as we are on tools, the surplus value theory is a sort of economic bomb which, if infused into action, could do unbelievable damage. Were the "justice" of that theory to be put into practice, we would probably be writing articles about why wages fall rather than why wages rise.

The problem of dividing the pie should be left to the free market of individual choices among employees and employers; consumers and producers; investors and borrowers; traders of all sorts, everywhere in exchange. If left to these free individuals, rather than becoming the handles of power in politics or among organizations representing any of these special interests, the decisions will be in the best interests of all.

Wherever the pie is divided by the free market, one thing seems sure: Marx's surplus value theory will be vetoed. For persons will continue, as they have over the past few centuries in our relatively free United States, to recognize a bargain when they see one. That bargain is tools. Of our total output, perhaps as much as 95 per cent is because of the use of tools. And this is at a cost of only about 15 per cent of total output, as pay to those who have saved to create these tools. That, and not Marx's concept, is the miracle that creates a surplus of value.

4. Tools To Harness Energy

All life on earth is developed, sustained, and powered by energy from the sun. And that is the beginning of the story of how man has harnessed energy to improve his level of living.

Man cannot use the sun's energy directly, except as it warms him and thus conserves the fuel already in his body for other uses. Were it possible to do this, the earth probably would be populated in unbelievable numbers; for the amount of energy coming from the sun is fantastically great.

Conversion of Solar Energy

Humans require a converter to change the sun's energy into usable forms. All human food comes directly or indirectly from plants which make direct use of the sun's energy in their growth. Plants are not, however, very efficient in doing this because about 10,000 units of the sun's energy are required to produce and store ten units of energy in the grown plant.[1]

Plants are in a sense, then, tools of mankind — the basic tools in man's life, without which there could be no human life as we know it. And as better plants can be found, they serve as better tools to raise man's welfare — raise his wages, in a sense.

---

[1]Estimate by the late Professor Raymond Lindeman of the University of Minnesota.

Some plants or parts of plants are eaten directly by humans. Others are eaten by herbivorous animal life, such as cattle; then we eat the cattle.

Herbivorous animals are not very efficient in storing energy, either. Of the ten energy units in the form of plants, said above to be produced from 10,000 units of the sun's energy, only one unit of energy is grown and stored in the animal; and not all of this is considered edible by humans. But we also consume animal products, such as milk and eggs, which add to the animal's efficiency somewhat.

So animals as well as plants serve us as tools, yielding a better life that is more to the human liking. And as more efficient animals can be found, that too raises wages, in a sense.

Some animals are carnivorous and live on other animals, of course. But they are few and mankind generally has domesticated none of them for use as food. They are too inefficient to compete with herbivorous animals, and so can hardly be classed among man's tools — except as a few are kept for pets to amuse us or for pulling an occasional dog-cart of very low energy efficiency.

Animal Power

In addition to being domesticated for purposes of food in a direct sense, animals also take the sun's energy that has been stored in plants and convert it into work, like tilling the soil, hauling loads, and the like. This process, in its time, was a great invention; for with the work of a horse, for instance, it became possible for a person to increase greatly his welfare — his wage.

According to Prentice, perhaps the greatest increase in

work efficiency from draft horses came with the invention of a collar to replace the throat strap.[2] This increased greatly the load the horse could pull. And there were other notable inventions of early days, such as the wheel to replace the dragged load and the "fifth wheel" by which to change the direction of four-wheeled vehicles.

Though highly important at the time of their discovery as compared with prior efficiency of human production, all these developments are rather unimportant in explaining the level of our present welfare. As we shall see, the present level comes mainly from other developments.

So back over time man has discovered how to use the energy from the sun, first in plant form as food and then, through plants, in the form of animals for food and for toil.

Another early form of releasing plant-stored energy was the burning of wood and other plant materials for cooking food and heating abodes. And later it was found that these plant materials of bygone days lay stored in the form of coal, oil, and gas. Because of the highly concentrated energy in these deposits, new uses eventually were developed whereby the heat was used for more direct sources of power.

Motive Power

Most important among these new uses of deposited plant-energy were methods of converting, first, heat energy and then other forms of energy into motion with which to propel vehicles and to drive moving parts. The heat from this stored energy also came to be used to reform and blend

[2]E. Parmalee Prentice. *Hunger and History*. Caldwell, Idaho: The Caxton Printers, Ltd., 1951. p. 50.

chemical materials into forms useful as tools. Thus it became possible to invent things like the steam engine and internal combustion engine. And in a somewhat different and new way, energy supplies were harnessed by using the water wheel to generate electricity, and more recently by the development of atomic energy.

These marvelous developments have now become commonplace in our lives. These, rather than the earlier forms of energy use, account for the major part of the increase in our productivity, from which higher and higher wages have been paid. These are responsible for almost all of the great difference in economic welfare between a huntsman or a man with a hoe — or even a man working with a horse or a buffalo — as compared with the income of the average wage earner in the United States today.

More Energy To Be Tapped

Yet all this has been accomplished with tools far from perfect in energy efficiency. Their efficiency is far superior, however, to that of the sun's energy going through plants to feed a horse, and then being turned into horse-fuel for plowing land on which to grow more plants for man to eat directly. By these newer means, the quantity of harnessed energy that may become used to do man's work is all but limitless. It is limited only by his foresight and restraint from immediate consumption, so as to be able to store his productivity in the form of more and still more tools. Then these can be put to work using more and still more of the limitless supply of the sun's energy.

This has been a simple description of the energy sources

for man's food and for his other wants over eons of time. It traces the development of the miracle of productivity in the United States and in other economically advanced countries. They are the result of ingenuity, savings, and the workpower of harnessed energy.

The Simple Idea of Tools

In essence, the formula is as simple as this: If a man can create a tool that makes it possible for him to produce in a day of work, say, twice as much of something as he could without the tool, he can have twice as much to enjoy. Or more accurately, he can have twice as much to enjoy *on a sustaining basis,* provided the machine makes it possible for him to produce double the output in enough less than a day's time so that he can also rebuild and replace whatever part of the machine was used up or worn out by the day's use.

If in addition to replacing the part of the machine he has worn out with the day's work he can also develop another tool that will further increase his output per hour, he can have even more to enjoy tomorrow. And so on, ad infinitum. If he is to accomplish this progressive improvement, he must restrain his current joys of consumption enough to make possible the development and accumulation of tools.

Output does not automatically increase, of course, merely because there have been some savings and their investment in new tools. If it were to take a day of work to make a tool which, by its use, would add only as much production as could have been produced in a day without the tool, then there would be no net gain in output. Tools are not productive per se but only as they add a *net* over-all increase.

Some misjudgments occur, of course, in efforts to develop tools in a free economy of private initiative. But errors there are at a minimum because the cost of the mistake can't be passed along to innocent bystanders as can be done in a controlled society.

So in a free society the growth in the development of energy-use measures, in a rough way, the harnessing of productive power. Horsepower-hours of energy output is one common measure.

In thinking of the effect of harnessed energy as an aid to men in their work, note that one horsepower is roughly equivalent to the energy of ten able-bodied men working strenuously — i.e., each man working an equivalent of lifting 55 pounds one foot a second, continuously. Or to illustrate its power another way, only one 75-watt light bulb in use represents as much energy as that of one man turning the crank on the generator.

The growth in energy output for the last century is shown in the accompanying table. A hundred years ago there was about half a horsepower of energy output for each hour of work, in addition to the energy of the worker himself. This — mostly by work animals — was equivalent to the help of five men. By 1950 the figure for horsepower-hours of additional help had risen to $3\frac{1}{3}$, or equivalent to the help of 33 men.

The use of nonliving sources of energy started to become important during the late nineteenth century, largely displacing work animals which now account for less energy than human labor itself. Nonlife sources now comprise the prime form of energy.

This help is not all clear gain in output, of course, because the efficiency is not 100 per cent. Some of the energy must

ENERGY OUTPUT, UNITED STATES
Horsepower-hours per man-hour of work

Year	Human labor	Work animals	Mineral fuels and water power	Total
1850	0.10	0.51	0.04	0.65
1860	0.10	0.56	0.04	0.70
1870	0.10	0.48	0.07	0.65
1880	0.10	0.48	0.12	0.70
1890	0.10	0.50	0.23	0.83
1900	0.10	0.49	0.36	0.95
1910	0.10	0.42	0.68	1.20
1920	0.10	0.36	1.29	1.75
1930	0.10	0.25	1.81	2.16
1940	0.10	0.18	2.48	2.76
1950	0.10	0.10	3.20	3.40

SOURCE: Calculations based on data in *America's Needs and Resources* by J. Frederic Dewhurst and Associates. New York: The Twentieth Century Fund. pp. 23 and 787. Also, Bureau of the Census, United States.

go to produce and replace the tools themselves. But after taking account of all that, it is a vital reason why wages are now five times what they were a century ago.[3]

How much better it is to have these silent, nonsuffering servants in the form of energy-using machines working for us than to have 33 human slaves! They far surpass slaves in efficiency of output, and with minimum upkeep costs. They don't rebel or run away. They are as willing to work as not to work.

This remarkable harnessing of energy, along with the idea of wage payments among specialists under relative freedom of exchange, accounts in great measure for the rise in wages in the United States over the decades.

---

[3]See Chapter 1, p. 9.

5. Doing What You Can Do Best

The creation and use of tools has been possible only because of a method of cooperation which has developed.

Apparently man is created in endless variety. We are told that no two persons are identical biologically. Nor are any two persons identical in their ability to do things, in their aptitudes of mind and body with which deeds are done and things are produced for economic betterment.

One person may be totally unable to do a thing that another can do; or if he can do it at all, it is with less ease and excellence. The cripple, for instance, is excluded from the fraternity of four-minute milers; probably Ginger Rogers is, too. Yet these persons are not without other rare abilities the four-minute miler lacks. Each sits in the bleachers observing with admiration the accomplishments of the other.

Many who have been carelessly labeled "handicapped" have been great scholars, composers, inventors. In those respects it is the rest of us who are handicapped. Everyone is handicapped, differing only in form or degree — differing endlessly, whether we think of it in the sense of abilities or in the sense of inabilities. Yet to be outstandingly gifted in more than one or a few respects is rare.

With this endless variation of abilities and inabilities, our enjoyments for living — beyond the many pleasures of the free things that exist in our natural environment — would be few indeed if we were all forced to live in isolation. In such an existence, the person unable to sing could have only the songs of the birds and the crickets, and the like, on the airwaves for his enjoyment. If he were unable to catch the wily fish, his dinners would all be fishless. His raiment would be only what he alone could fashion from materials he was able to gather or capture. And only the few devices he could invent would be his to use.

Personal isolation would be an existence of meager means at best. It would reflect our inabilities in a dominant fashion, revealing vividly both the fact and some of the consequences of human variation.

An unfortunate consequence of endless human variation is to create the opportunity for endless misunderstanding. But the other side — the bright side — of the same coin is one of opportunity. It creates the chance for endless cooperation, to the mutual advantage of participants. This opportunity can exist only as differences are understood and tolerated — allowed to blossom into the cooperation with which we are here concerned.

We may reap fruits of human variation and enjoy things not of our own direct creation only if we discover how to allow this cooperation to work. It springs from trees whose roots are hidden from our view and appreciation.

What One Can Do Best

What happens under this form of cooperation may be seen by a simple illustration. Suppose two persons are living an isolated existence. Let us say that they have aptitudes that are totally unlike. What one can produce or do well the other cannot do at all, and vice versa. Each can produce many times as much of his own product as he has any use for. And yet his taste for the other's product is equal to that for his own.

It is clear that if each produces double his own wants, exchanging his surplus with the other, they can both double their consumption level of products they enjoy. They could, in effect, double their wages through the simple process of exchanging half for half of what they produce.

Now suppose that instead of being a society of two persons, it is a society of three persons of this same design, each of whom can produce many times his own use of his product. By the simple process of triangular exchange of what they produce, each of them could treble his consumption of products he enjoys. This is the same as increasing wages.

Similarly, for a society of four persons, five persons, and so on.

A Seeming Miracle

This process of exchanging the fruits of one's efforts performs what may seem like a miracle. Each is allowed to use more fully his peculiar abilities in production. The appearance of a miracle is due to the fact that the whole seems greater than the sum of its parts — more economic enjoyment from working together in this way than from existing in isolation. By voluntarily cooperating in this manner everyone can benefit who will join in the process.[1]

The seeming miracle does not really arise from any in-

---

[1]For further discussion on this point, see *Government — An Ideal Concept* by Leonard E. Read. Irvington-on-Hudson, N. Y.: The Foundation for Economic Education, Inc., 1954. Especially pp. 17-31.

crease in ability to produce, however. This ability remains the same for each person as it was at birth, in endless variety. True, we do not know the full limits of our abilities and may fail to develop them to the fullest extent; on the other hand, we may overestimate our abilities and may, as a consequence, limit in various ways the welfare of ourselves and others. But in spite of this, our abilities are those inherent at birth and the seeming miracle occurs for another reason.

What really happens is that by rearranging — through exchange — the products which the peculiar talents of each has made available, there is opened up an outlet for untold amounts of specialized production. Take these written words, for instance. My own demand for them is such that they probably would never have been produced except that others might want them. So something practically useless to me became available for exchange with someone who wants it. It may be some person unknown to me on whose farm is produced the egg I had for breakfast — perhaps a farmer who produces six thousand eggs a day and who himself eats only two of them.

That is how the seeming miracle works. It is really rooted in exchange rather than in production. It is a process that allows rearrangement of what is produced from the producer, who wants it little or not at all, to someone who wants it much more as a consumer. So there arises a cooperating circle of such exchanges.

The total of production is still no more than the sum of its parts, in the sense that total production is only what separate persons have produced. Nothing is produced except what somebody produces, by individual, separate, personal effort. But by the miracle of exchange a person may become able to trade the fruit of an hour of his own labor for what would take him ten or a hundred or a million hours to produce himself — if he could produce it at all. He trades with others who gain a similar advantage from the exchange.

So the seeming miracle of exchange, yielding untold increases in the usefulness of things, is easily and almost effortlessly accomplished by the simple and easy process of trading.

It all comes about without people having to work longer hours. They probably work even fewer hours when any economy becomes more and more developed in this way, under the process of specialization and exchange. They work fewer hours than if it were an economy of privation, not so developed. Leisure becomes a luxury they can now better afford, so they accept more leisure in the market for their time. The process, rather than to demand more mental or physical effort in the form of work, only increases the extent of concentration of one's effort on what he can do best. He spends less time on what he cannot do well, obtaining it instead by means of trade.

In this way he produces far more. The increase is not directly that of his own appraisal of its worth to himself, but reflects how others appraise it for themselves by access in the market. So we trade our special abilities — trade our peculiarities, so to speak, and make of them an economic virtue instead of a vice.

Limits on the Process

The only limits to the extent wages can be increased by this process are these:

    1. There is, of course, a limit to what a person — even

the most talented — can produce. The more capable he is in a rare ability, the higher this ceiling becomes.

2. There is a limit on his ability to find other interested traders with products they have produced beyond their own wants.

3. There are geographic and other barriers to exchange throughout the whole of society.

These three factors set the ceiling on the possible rise. Only as these barriers have been removed has it been possible for wages to rise to the point where they now are.

Barriers are in many instances the result of government intervention in production affairs, in the market, and in devices for exchange. But it is not the purpose here to discuss them in detail.

If wages are to be increased further, these problems must receive attention. The capacity to increase one's specialized production beyond one's own needs includes all the aids to specialized production discussed in previous chapters — savings, the creation of tools, the harnessing of power, and the like. These become aids to the use of a person's rare ability, putting increased leverage on the unusual ability of a person like an inventor or a machine technician. By specialized work in a highly complex exchange society, one person can spend a lifetime perfecting his unusual aptitude for doing some almost indistinguishable little bit of the production process, for some complex machine sold all over the world.

One would be remiss, however, if he did not recognize certain hazards in this seeming miracle of division of labor in a complex, specialized economy of exchange.

First, though there are material benefits from such specialization, there can be serious consequences outside the material realm. A man who prepares himself for an extreme specialty and concentrates upon it for a livelihood, tends to that extent to become a physical, mental, and spiritual victim of the narrow confines of his specialty. He need not be so enslaved to his specialty, to be sure, and may be able to escape its restrictive tendencies. But the danger in this respect is certainly greater than for his ancestor whose living depended on a wider practice of various arts.

Thomas Davidson once told of a man who had ladled tar with such accomplishment for over thirty years that in his mind he might not be able to make a living if the demand for tar ladling should disappear. To that man, his perfection of a specialty had made him the victim of an insecure reliance upon a narrow specialty.

By contrast, a noted surgeon of my acquaintance had mastered nine trades before entering medical training. This gave him a great feeling of security that the tar ladler lacked. In like manner, a pioneer — despite his modest material living — evidences a spirit of self-reliance which is some compensation for his lack of economic welfare.

Specialization Can Be Overdone

So it is well to do many things, outside one's vocation if not within it, for nonmaterial reasons as well as from the standpoint of revealing talents that have been latent. Even at the cost of some possible economic gain, some of one's time and effort may well be devoted to repairing the intellectual and moral loss that sometimes is the price of specialization. In becoming a wealthy giant in pursuing one's most rare talents, one must not dwarf and cripple oneself in all other respects. Not all means of satisfaction are composed of economic wealth, and there is no market in which you can buy nonmaterial welfare with material means. And so a man who would be wholesomely free must think of these dangers, as well as of the economic fruits of specialization.

Second, in addition to the narrowing tendency of increased specialization on one's culture and interests, there is also the danger of losing the material welfare we have attained by undermining the processes which have made it possible to rise to present levels. Our economic welfare could fall by removing the means of its attainment. If persons should be prohibited from producing their specialties, or from trading them with others in the markets of the world, the fall could parallel the rise we have enjoyed.

6. The Lubricant For Exchange

In the market we find persons trading the fruits of their special abilities with one another. Each does whatever economic task he can do best. He creates a surplus beyond his own needs. He then trades this with others who are in a similar position of surplus, having things he wants. So by trading rather than by working harder, both sides of the exchange greatly increase the satisfaction of their wants. Human differences can in this way be made to yield a more bounteous living for every participant.

Yet there is another important aspect of trading to be considered, too. It involves an aid to trade, without which our high and rising wages would not be possible.

Two men living in an isolated society of their own will find the trading of their specialties easy to arrange and to carry out. All they need do is meet and arrive at the terms of the trade, and then make the physical transfer of the goods. The magnet of mutual benefit draws them together for a deal.

From being a simple matter in this society of only two persons, the process of direct trading of goods for goods becomes increasingly difficult, if not impossible, when the number increases to three, then four, and eventually to two billion persons.

Let me illustrate. I enjoy tea. Yet I know not a single person who produces any. And even if I did know someone, perhaps he would not want what I have for sale. Most likely he has no appetite whatever for words from my pen, for instance. So the two of us cannot trade our products directly. The difference between what we produce and what each wants causes a sort of friction that precludes a trade. So our offerings will not move in trade until an alternative outlet — perhaps involving a sort of lubricant to remove this friction — can be found.

Now suppose a third party who has sugar for sale wants to buy some of my written words. And suppose the tea producer wants sugar. Now we have a sort of lubricant that will let all three products move in trade. The sugar man trades me his sugar for my words; then I trade the sugar with the tea producer for his tea. Everybody thus obtains what he wants, whereas previously we had been unable to do so.

Money Enters Trade

If the third man had entered the market with money instead of with sugar, the trade would have been even easier to arrange. With money acceptable to all, the man with the money could have traded with either of us initially, whichever was the most convenient for any reason. He could have bought my words; then, with the money, I could have bought the tea. Or he could have first bought the tea; then he and I could have traded tea for words.

This, in essence, is the function of money. It serves as a lubricant in exchange — a medium of exchange. Persons who do not want it for itself alone will accept it as an intermediate step to getting what they want in the trading process. Serving in a sense like a lubricant in a motor, money facilitates the movement of other things in exchange without itself

44

being consumed or even wanted for consumption. Money does not serve as the end product in the satisfaction of human wants — except perhaps for the miser who may hoard some and gloat over its possession as one would prize a picture or an antique. In which case, the miser holds some of it as a commodity rather than as money per se, and to that extent it is no longer money.

In the earlier illustration where the sugar man entered trade, the sugar itself served temporarily as money and thereafter reverted to a commodity. It came to rest with the tea man for purposes of being consumed. This illustrates how it is possible for a "money commodity" to serve either one or the other of these two functions, at different times and places.

Had I for any reason doubted that the sugar would be acceptable to someone who had tea for sale, the sugar could not have served to lubricate the trade. It was necessary for me to accept its acceptability by others whose products I wanted, else I would have refused it in trade for purposes of money. So for anything to be accepted and to serve as money, the decision is not restricted to the desire for it by only one person. It is unlike strawberries which one person may prize whether any other person likes them or not. For anything to serve as money, it must enjoy a multiple acceptance; otherwise it cannot perform the task of money. And the wider its acceptance, the better it will serve as a lubricant for trade.

A Great Invention

Money is perhaps the greatest economic invention of all time. It lubricates the vast economic mechanism of trade which could not operate without it. It allows a deal to be made

45

between persons unknown to each other, because of distance or some other reason.

By using money, the two persons don't need to find each other directly. Instead, every producer puts his goods and services into a vast stream of trade, getting money in return. Then he puts the money back into the market to get what he really wants.

The producer does not know — nor does he care, really — to whom his product goes for consumption. Neither does he know nor care who produced the item he consumes or uses. It is all done behind the curtain of money exchanges in a trading economy. The only person who need be contacted is the one person at the point of trading contact. And even this can be quite impersonal. Witness, for instance, the unknown sources of all the things in a department store, or in a mail order catalog.

That is why money is such a great invention. That is why it serves so efficiently as a lubricant for exchanging the specialties of production all over the world, between widely separated persons in remote locations. The Yukon fur draped over the shoulders of a Park Avenue lady, or a mahogany table in the home of a wheat farmer in some remote part of Canada, can be explained only as an accomplishment made possible by money.

A great advantage of money, so far as wage earners are concerned, is that it is a device that reduces all alternative offerings of employment to one common denominator of expression — the money wages of the various job offerings. Comparison is then much easier than if the pay offer were in one case a certain number of bushels of wheat, in another some shoes, and the like.

Different Moneys

The more people accept one money the world over, the better that money will lubricate trade. Ideally there would be but one money enjoying universal acceptance. Then all trade could pass through one medium. And in this way, goods and services produced in abundance as specialties all over the world could, so far as money is concerned, enjoy the widest possible access to those who want them.

All sorts of things have served as money in exchange — such as cattle, shells, silver, gold, copper, aluminum, paper. In Europe during World War II, nylon hose and cigarettes became important as money.

But it is not relevant to this discussion to wonder why different things have served as money. It is sufficient to note that separate and competing monies will continue until and unless the "ideal money" is found; until and unless something gains enough common acceptance and understanding so that nobody can adulterate its use and destroy its usefulness as money; until and unless neither politician nor any other person can gain the power to tamper with money for his personal gain.

Adulterating the Lubricant

For purposes of our present problem, we shall only observe that we operate with an imperfect money system. We do not now have an ideal money, nor are we even threatened with this blessing for the foreseeable future. And so it is important to note the effect on wages of an imperfect lubricant of exchange, which we now have.

When you accept money in trade, you are proceeding on faith in it as a sort of implied contract. The implied contract is this: When you trade something for money as an intermediate step to getting what you eventually want in exchange, you are operating on the assumption that the money will serve your intent rather than thwart it.

Let us say, for instance, that you accept money as an intermediate step between your bushel of wheat and the two bushels of corn you want. You might have traded direct, but you preferred to use money as a go-between. So you sell the wheat for two dollars in money; then you buy the corn for one dollar a bushel, or two dollars for the two bushels. While the money was in your possession, it was your expectation that nothing would be done to money to alter its worth in terms of the wheat or the corn. So far as the money is concerned, you expect it to retain worth in exchange equivalent to one bushel of wheat or two bushels of corn. That is the nature of the contract implied in one's use of money *as money*. Your use of it is not for the purpose of speculating in the worth of money per se.

Yet the worth of a unit of our present money is subject to constant change. Under inflation it becomes worth less — prices rise — unless there are offsetting influences to be ignored here.

The Counterfeit Gains

In the illustration, if there is inflation, the two dollars you received for your wheat would lose some of its worth while you held the money, and would then buy less than the full two bushels of corn that you had presumed to be its worth under the implied contract. You still have the two dollars, of course, but as a result of inflation the corn has risen above one dollar a bushel. Through no overt act of your own, you lose some of the worth of your property. So would everyone else who was then holding money or money claims.

Who would gain, if all these persons lose? The gains go to the diluters of the money — a counterfeiter, perhaps, or the government, either by a direct act of its own or by a grant of permit to someone. They gain by getting some money without producing anything in the usual sense; by getting something for nothing while the sufferers lose some worth of their money and money claims. Then as a consequence of inflation, various other persons gain or lose through effects that alter the essence of all sorts of contractual deals.

Inflation and Wages

Inflation affects wage earners directly in two principal ways:

First, since the wage earner gets essentially all his income as a money income, his money then loses worth. His pay will lose worth while he keeps it as money or in the form of some money equivalent. Even while he holds his pay check it loses worth, though this is an insignificant amount of loss for those who spend their pay quickly. Only in a panic stage of inflation, like that of Germany in 1923 or of China in the mid-forties, can it be much of a factor while one holds a pay check for a day or two. In China, for instance, when money was said to lose half its worth every two weeks, the loss would be a few per cent by one who held his pay check one day.

Second, it affects the worth of his pension funds, his life insurance, his bonds, and other such forms of savings that are money contracts. Their loss of worth can be extremely serious, both in degree and in timing. It can become serious in degree because of the cumulative effect of continuing inflation. If a dollar loses 10 per cent of its worth each year as compared with the previous year, there will remain only twelve cents of its worth at the end of twenty years.

But more important than either of these, in a sense, is the illusion of welfare that inflation creates. This can lead to serious consequences. Whenever a person is less well off than he thinks he is, he is likely to be headed for considerable trouble.

For instance, a wage of eight dollars an hour, after the twenty years of inflation at the rate of 10 per cent each year, is no better than a dollar an hour without the inflation. If one is fooled by this and raises his level of living from one to eight, or to four, or even to a 1.01, he will be living beyond his means.

Inflation also seriously affects such things as wage contracts extending into the future. Insofar as inflation alters the implied contract assumed by those who hold money — namely, that it will continue of equal worth — its violation also becomes reflected in every monetary contract like a wage contract. As the worth of money is reduced by inflation, the burden of a contracted wage rate is also reduced. This violates, in a sense, the implication in the contract when it was negotiated. To protect against this, some wage contracts are being designed to include an increase to take care of assumed inflation. Inflation thus becomes a legally vested interest in contract form, throwing the weight of sentiment on the side of continuing the inflation. Can inflation ever be stopped that way?

The Clipped Dollars

Over a period of years, money wages in the United States have risen for two reasons — (1) increased production, in which wages have shared, and (2) inflation. The first adds buying power. But the second is an illusory gain because inflation merely adds more dollars of less buying power. And the extent of the inflation illusion has been great.

Suppose, for instance, that a man now due to retire at age 65 began work when he was 20. And suppose, to simplify our problem, he had never advanced in skills beyond swimming with the tide of the over-all increase in productivity, so that his wage went with the average for all private employment during the period. His money wage per hour now would be more than seven times what it was in 1910. Had there been no inflation, however, his wage would presumably have risen to a little less than three times what it was in 1910, not seven times.

Or if we compare his present wage with that of a quarter century ago, it is now two and one-half times as high as it was then. Considerably more than half of this rise has been an illusory wage increase of inflation, reducing the worth of the dollar.

So for nearly half a century now, inflation has put more dollars into the pay check than have come from increased productivity. Inflation is not real dollars in the sense of buying power, like the ones arising from increased productivity. They seem nice to have, and they look exactly like the other dollars. But these added dollars really buy nothing, as against having avoided inflation with its addition of worthless dollars that go into the pay check.

Inflation, then, does not raise real wages. It only creates the illusion of rising wages.

Though somewhat beyond the scope of this analysis, it should be observed that the government controls money. It is therefore government which inflates the money, or allows it to be inflated under controls such as the monetary standard, the reserve requirements, and interest rates. And so, in this sense, government must be held responsible for creating the illusory wage rate which accompanies inflation.

A Major Disaster

My final point is to suggest the disaster that would come upon us if, through inflation and deflation, the efficiency of the lubricant for exchange should be retarded, or the money system destroyed. What if violent changes should turn money from a lubricant into an object of speculation? For when persons hoard money in anticipation that it will gain worth, or avoid it because of anticipation that it will lose worth, this miraculous lubricant cannot do its work. Then catastrophe would be upon our highly geared economy. Then the usual progress which causes real wages to rise could no longer operate, until and unless a new lubricant were found and installed.

We are interested here in why wages rise, in a real sense rather than in an illusory sense. It behooves all of us who want continued progress, therefore, to become greatly concerned about this threat of inflation. This means searching out the underlying cause of why governments either want to inflate money or feel impelled to do so, then correcting the cause.

7. Contracting For Progress

Money, the lubricant for exchange, makes widespread trade possible. Without it our present high level of wages could hardly have come to be. Yet, serious inflation and deflation can cause money to lose its capacity to lubricate exchange.

Inflation mixes worthless dollars with the sound dollars of a productive economy. The dollars inflation puts into pay envelopes add nothing but higher price tags on things.[1]

As inflation becomes blended with the real buying power of production, dollars of diluted worth are the result. You can buy less at the counter with one of them. Not only is the worth of the dollar diluted, but understanding about the source of progress also is distorted by the illusion of inflation.

Rich Uncles and Welfare

Inflation fools us into a false sense of welfare. Perhaps the illusion comes about in some such manner as the following:

Suppose a wage earner has an industrious and thrifty uncle who remembers him in his will. At the uncle's demise the wage earner gains buying power, dollar for dollar in proportion to the amount of the inheritance. Everyone knows that.

If this happens to two people, both of them will gain in like manner. Or three. Or four.

---

[1]Inflation is an increase in the quantity of money, not a rise in prices which is only the consequence of inflation.

And so it seems at first blush that if only this could happen on a national scale, everyone would benefit in like manner. But who will serve as the universal uncle? Our common uncle, Uncle State, of course.

Most uncles die only once, and an inheritance once received can never be repeated. But the State, on the other hand, has innumerable lives to give to its needy nephews and nieces. It seems able to grant them a sort of inheritance over and over again. The State, however, is confronted with the problem of a source for the funds it gives, since the State is without economic means itself. So the State must first collect from its nephews and nieces the substance of the repeated "inheritances" to be given back to them.

Inflation Is a Tax

Inflation is one way the State obtains these funds. And thus the buying power of money is diluted with these inflation dollars, which become the source of the inheritances from Uncle State.

The nephews and nieces, of course, are no better off as a result.[2] Somewhere there has been a slip of reasoning betwixt one person's rich uncle and an uncle without means for all of us. The clue to the answer lies in the fact that such benefits can come only out of production; that without production there can be no benefits.

The singular rich uncle was productive and thrifty. He saved up buying power by foregoing consumption over the years. And it was title to that real, productive wealth which became yours at the time of his demise.

---

[2]They are worse off, in fact, but the reasons are beyond the scope of this discussion.

If Uncle State, on the other hand, tries to give all of us enough to live on for the rest of our lives so that we could retire, who would produce the things for us to live by? Therein lies the catch in such a scheme for general welfare. For if nothing is produced, we would have nothing to live on from these promises to be financed by inflation.

Were we all to receive in like manner half enough, presumably, to live on and were all to half retire, we could have only half a living — the half we produced. The inflation inheritance of half a living would, likewise, give us nothing.

And for lesser degrees of inflation, the same would be true. We can have only what is produced, no more and no less. For production is the only thing that gives either wages or inheritance their substance. Money dilution for any purpose merely causes the price tags to go higher and higher.

That is the real danger of the inflation illusion. And we can't live on the substance of an illusion — full time or half time or a minute a day, now or in old age. In trying to live beyond the means produced and available, tragedy will surely ensue in one form or another.

One exceedingly foreboding form that this inflation illusion seems to be taking has to do with wage agreements. In important respects these contracts amount to an attempt to contract for progress. The certain consequences of any such attempt at the impossible should give us deep concern.

Let me illustrate.

A Wage Contract for My Boy

In the year 2012, the Lord willing, my boy will be old enough to retire at age 65. He will then be in the final year of what I hope will have been a worthy occupational life, just prior to being forced to retire.

Here is a proposal. Let us say that I want to help him by bargaining for his wage for that year — the year 2012. As his representative at this collective bargaining table, I shall herewith state my proposal and give my reasons for my demands. Then if anyone will accept the offer, we shall see if we can work out the other minor details of the agreement.

My proposal is that you pay him a wage of $29.99 per hour for the year 2012.

This figure is arrived at by the same method now coming into vogue in negotiations over wage contracts. Contracts are being offered for a period of five years, or perhaps more. What I am proposing is merely to extend the idea of these five-year contracts, on the theory that if a principle is good for five years, it is even better for 56 years. Eleven times better for 56 years than for five years? Well, better, anyhow.

My proposal is based on the actual record of wages over the past working generation. I have merely taken trends since a man now ready to retire started work on reaching age 21, and extended them on to the year 2012 on a strictly mathematical basis.

Beginning with the present average wage rate for all laborers in the petroleum and coal industries ($2.52 per hour), I first added the average yearly rate of increase in productivity since 1910 (2.2 per cent).[3] Since increases in productivity have appeared in wage rates more or less in full, this step would seem to have ample precedent.

---

[3]In calculating the $29.99 rate, I am assuming that in the year 2012 his work will correspond to that of present laborers in the petroleum and coal industries.

REAL AND UNREAL WAGE RATES
Hourly wage rates, United States

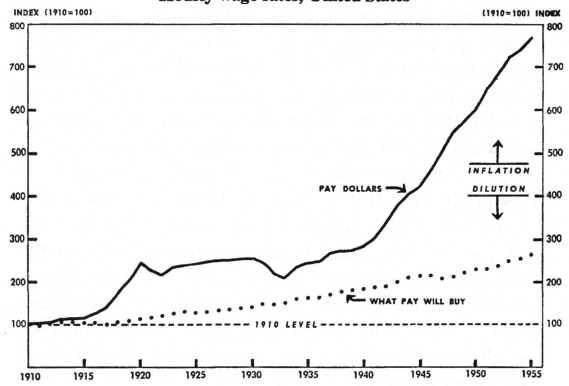

SOURCE: Real wage column derived from *Employment and Wages in the United States* by W. S. Woytinski & Associates, Twentieth Century Fund, p. 586; *Economic Report to the President,* January 1956, p. 191. Nominal wage column derived from Woytinski, *op. cit.,* p. 585; *Economic Report to the President, op. cit.,* p. 208.

Next, the dollar has lost buying power over this period at a rate which, unless wages had risen enough to offset it, would have almost exactly canceled out all the increase from productivity. Except as this loss in buying power of the dollar was offset by wage increases, labor would be no better off now than a generation ago; except for such an adjustment in wages, wage dollars would have lost buying power about in proportion to the increase in productivity. So I am adding an inflation factor to my demands, based on past experience for nearly half a century.

57

These two factors give me my figure of $29.99 an hour for the year 2012, which I am proposing for a contract.

You may feel that you would be taking too great a risk in accepting such an offer, because productivity and inflation may not continue to go up for the next working generation as fast as they have in the one just past. True. But it is also true that they may go up even faster; that is the risk my son would be taking in signing such a contract. Do not these risks offset one another — yours vs. his — at this figure of $29.99? To equalize risks in this way would seem fair enough.

You may argue that you are opposed to inflation. But to that I would reply that you can do nothing about inflation all by yourself; that you have been opposed to it in the past, too, but that it has existed in spite of you; that holding your hands up against the wind will not stop it, so you might just as well take inflation as a fact and proceed to adjust yourself to it accordingly.

The Way To Begin

You may argue that if everyone takes this attitude of not opposing inflation by every means at his command, merely because he can't do anything about it alone, nobody will ever do anything about it; that only the combined efforts of enough persons who want to do something about it will ever terminate inflation; that one thing you can do, for sure, is to avoid becoming a contractor for future inflation by writing the assumption of its continuance into your wage and other contracts; that *you can't fight inflation if you become a vested interest in its behalf, as in such a wage contract.*

At this point in our bargaining I am ready to concede the

force of these objections. And so I shall withdraw my offer of any such contract, urging all other wage bargainers to avoid such a scheme, too.

From the standpoint of the welfare of wage earners, such a general pattern of wage contracts is sheer folly. Some even question seriously putting both an assumed increase in productivity as well as a "cost of living" clause into long-term wage contracts. But this scheme is far worse. It not only contracts for a progressive increase in productivity at a predetermined rate; but in addition, it guarantees a continuous rise in the cost of living, in effect.

General wage agreements such as this would merely entrench inflation as a contractual way of life. This is true whether the agreement extends to the year 2012, or to 1961, or to 1957. The longer the period contracted on any such basis, the more serious its threat to the stability and progress of our economy.

The Erosion of Savings

Were I to argue the danger, and bargain for built-in inflation in the wage contract on some such basis, another problem arises to plague me.

My son, let us assume, wants to become self-responsible in his old age. He wants to provide for his elderly freedom and independence by saving enough during his working years to take care of his needs after retirement. How can he do this?

Let us first appraise his problem under the assumption that there were to be no inflation and no increase in productivity — that wage rates were to be stable, in other words. And let us also assume that my son wants to plan for a retirement income equal to half his working wage of $2.52 an hour. He is to provide for an income after retirement amounting to $2,620.80 a year, let us say.[4]

In order to provide for this sum on retirement, he would have to save and invest in a pension fund at the rate of $353.81 a year for the entire period. This would be 6¾ per cent of his income.[5]

Buying Power Diminished

If, on the other hand, inflation were to be built into the wage structure in the manner previously explained, my son would have to save at a much higher rate. For instance, a dollar saved during his first year of work would, in the first year after retirement, amount to only 38 cents in buying power, as a result of the inflation. This means that he would have had to put in $2.65 during his first working year in order to have, on retirement, the buying power that one dollar would have had without the inflation.

So why not add enough to the $29.99 rate to cover the loss of buying power of the wage earner's savings? Since the loss was due to inflation, why not charge it to inflation? Why not add it to wages, as was done with the inflation factor explained earlier?

If this were done, it would merely mean that still higher prices would result, cutting even further into the value of savings for retirement. This, in turn, would call for adding even more to the wage for the same reason. And so forth.

---

[4]Based on 40-hour week and vacations with pay.

[5]Figures provided by a leading insurance company. The plan is the usual pension plan, invested mainly in bonds, mortgages, and the like.

An endless process would have been set in motion, like a cat hopelessly chasing its bobtail at an ever-increasing speed.

This pursuit of something for nothing by means of inflation is a fruitless search that can yield nothing to the general welfare of wage earners. Time and effort and hopes spent on it are wasted from gainful pursuits.

Inflation in France

This wasted effort and false hope, of contracting inflation into higher wages, should especially concern the wage earner. To see why, we need only review earlier historical experiences with their tragic ending of the inflation act.

In speaking of the consequences of inflation at the time of the French Revolution, Andrew Dickson White said:

> Now began to be seen more plainly some of the many ways in which an inflation policy robs the working class . . . . the classes living on fixed incomes and small salaries felt the pressure first, as soon as the purchasing power of their fixed incomes was reduced. Soon the great class living on wages felt it even more sadly . . . . the demand for labor was diminished; laboring men were thrown out of employment . . . the price of labor . . . went down. . . . Workmen of all sorts were more and more thrown out of employment.[6]

So if the wage earner is to be able to enjoy further increases in *real* wages through a healthy and sound economic growth, inflation must be stopped. But inflation can never be stopped if it becomes entrenched in the wage structure as a contractual way of life. It can never be stopped if wage contracts are

[6]White, Andrew Dickson. *Fiat Money Inflation in France*. Irvington-on-Hudson, N. Y.: The Foundation for Economic Education, Inc., 1952, pp. 32, 65-66.

so designed that employers and employees come to have a divided and conflicting interest in meeting the common enemy of inflation.

Progress cannot be built on an inflation bubble. It cannot be built on a raise in wages offset by a decline in what a dollar of wage will buy. For then the welfare of wage earners will burst when the inflation bubble bursts, hurting them especially.

8. The Cost Of Being Governed

Wages have been spoken of as though they were entirely composed of money in the pay envelope which you could spend as you wish. They have been discussed as though each dollar could be spent for a loaf of your favorite brand of bread, or for peanuts, or for a new car; or given to your church, or to your favorite charity; or turned over to your wife to spend as she deems wise; or whatever.

But this ignores an important fact. Not all your wages are available to you for free choice of spending in this way.

If you produce in your garden twice the fruits and vegetables this year that you did last year, you have twice the "gardening wage." Or if yours is a commercial garden and you have sold twice the amount of produce, you have twice the income and can buy twice the amount of things of your choice.

Let us suppose that this year you produce 20 bushels of potatoes worth $2.50 a bushel, after taking out costs other than pay for your own time. You have a $50.00 total wage. Having worked 50 hours, you have an hourly wage of $1.00.

Now if I had come along in the spring and offered my help at a wage of $50.00 for the season, and if together we produced 40 bushels instead of 20, our wage would still be $1.00 an hour — $100 for 100 hours.

But suppose that instead of offering my services to grow an additional 20 bushels of potatoes, I had offered to guard your potato patch against the mountain lions for a seasonal fee of $50.00. You would, of course, have turned my offer down for two reasons: (1) There are no mountain lions around anyhow, and what I am offering is no more a service to you than it would be for me to guard the mountain lions against your potatoes. (2) To pay me that high a wage would require all the proceeds from the potatoes you produce, leaving you nothing as pay for your own exercise.

Service Charges by Fiat

But suppose I had bargained on a different basis, and said: "Since the protection of the potato patch is important to both of us, I will chip in along with you and pay an equal share of the cost of this general welfare. In other words, I will do all the work of protecting the patch and you will do all the other work of raising the potatoes. Then we will each pay half of each other's income in return for half the product — each of us getting, at the end of the year, ten bushels of potatoes plus half of the service of having had them protected."

This would still be unappealing to you, since the protection is worth nothing to you and you would not pay anything for it willingly. Why give up half your potatoes for nothing?

Let us assume, however, that by some device — though we are not here considering that device — it is decreed that this protection is "necessary"; that it must be provided for the "general welfare." That decree overrules your objection without answering it. And so I become hired by decree. Under this situation we find that wages are still nominally at a level of $1.00 per hour for both of us. Yet the worth of the wage has been changed. Though nominally the same wage

64

as before, when all the time of both of us was spent raising potatoes, it can't possibly be worth as much as before because we have produced less.

A wage can buy no more than is produced. And under this new arrangement the two of us have produced only half as much as before, or 20 bushels instead of 40 bushels of potatoes. So our wages will now buy only 20 bushels of potatoes — plus protection against the mountain lions, of course. Our wages have in this instance, then, lost buying power in proportion to that part over which there was loss of free choice in spending — half the total yearly wage of our little community. The loss was the amount of forced purchase of a service worth nothing to you.

Nor would this loss of buying power have been eliminated by diluting our money to the extent of the protection cost. This would only have raised prices sharply for the reduced amount of production. No matter what is done to the money, only a miracle can turn 20 bushels of potatoes into 40 bushels.

Uncertain Worth of Forced Sales

An extreme illustration has been given, to be sure. But it suggests clearly the principle that is involved.

Not all services are as worthless as guarding your potato patch against the mountain lions. I might, instead, have offered to pick the bugs off your potatoes. If this de-bugging had produced 20 or more additional bushels of potatoes at a cost of $50.00 — and lacking a way to do the same thing more cheaply — my offer would have been acceptable to you. You would willingly have hired me, because my service would have been worth the cost to you.

My point is that if you are forced to buy certain "goods" or a "service" priced by edict, you are an enslaved buyer. Under these circumstances, what you are forced to pay has no necessary relationship to what it is worth to you. It may be worth nothing. It may, in fact, be of negative worth to you — something you would gladly pay to avoid rather than to have. Or it may, on the other hand, be worth something to you. It may be worth a little bit. Or it may be worth any amount up to the decreed price you are forced to pay. It may conceivably be worth more than the decreed price, rarely and for a few persons.

So in such an instance you can't escape a purchase at a price unrelated to its worth to you. You are not allowed to go without it, nor to produce it yourself, nor to buy it from a more efficient source. This means that the "income" required to pay for it is likewise of uncertain worth. It is worthless because you attach no worth at all to what you get in return. At best, it is income of less worth than any other dollar of your income, which can be spent for what you most want to buy.

The Nature of Government Services

The costs of government are of this type for individual persons in the nation. These costs are all paid with compulsory taxes of one form or another. Since each service is of uncertain worth to any individual person, therefore the income from which the taxes are paid is of uncertain worth to that person.

Government is concerned with governing. It means to govern, to control, to rule, to exercise authority.

Or put it this way: A political government is an agency we set up to govern ourselves. It operates outside and beyond those things we do for ourselves individually, as we voluntarily cooperate with one another in willing exchange and trade.

A political government does not do all the governing, of course. Banks and other businesses have private policemen, guards, and night watchmen. Organizations of all sorts have governing bodies which in some degree govern their members; sometimes these organizations attempt to govern outsiders, too. There is even a bit of governing within each family; witness the posterior pains of childhood.

A Monopoly Power

The distinctive feature of the political governmental body is its monopoly status, its compulsory "sales" to every member of the society. This is not true of most other forms of governing within our society. We may escape them in one way or another. If we do not like the private policeman in one bank, for instance, we can take our business elsewhere. It may be less easy for a child to leave his family, but small boys still go over the hill at times.

Our concern with the matter of governing is its relation to our judgment of its worth. This affects real wages. And that is why the monopoly of political government is of a special type — of special concern.

The total cost of political government in the United States is now about a hundred billion dollars a year. Were you to appraise each part of this enormous expenditure in order to judge its worth to you, as you would your individual grocery

WAGE TRENDS IN THE UNITED STATES
Buying power before and after taxes

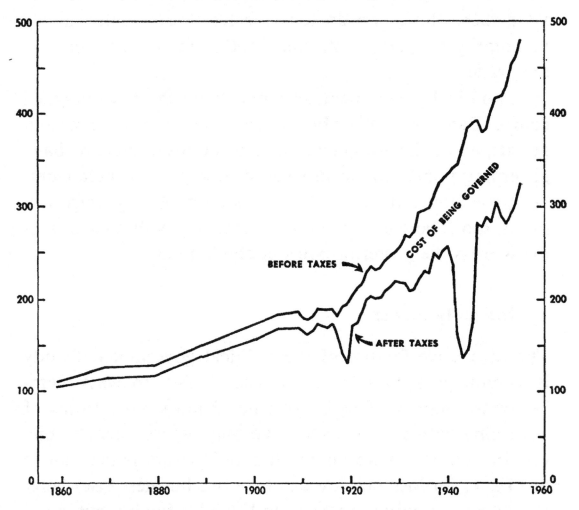

SOURCE: For wages before taxes, see Chapter 1. The cost of being governed was derived from data on government costs and personal incomes, by the United States Department of Commerce.

purchases or the selection of a necktie, you would find yourself confronted with an almost inconceivable task. For were you to study the things which government does and judge their worth in this way, even at the hasty and superficial rate of one million dollars an hour, you would not be able to finish until well into the twenty-first century. Besides, since persons do not agree on that any more than they do about the worth of items in a department store or mail order catalog, I don't know just what these things are worth. Nor do you, I dare say. All we can say is that it is a monopoly market costing the average family about $2,000 a year to be governed. These are service charges we must pay — or go to jail.

It seems certain, then, that the value of our present political government is completely uncertain for any one person and, therefore, for all persons combined. We can't possibly know its worth, so long as a given service remains a monopoly that individuals are compelled to purchase. All we know, for any one item, is that it is still tolerated by a majority of the vocal citizens.

Effect on Wage Rates

One would be remiss not to think of the worth of government when he is appraising the worth of his wages. The part of his wages going for political government today is of quite a different sort of worth from the remainder, which he can spend for objects of his choice and preference. It is quite different, dollar for dollar, from income he can use to buy whatever appeals to him as cheapest and best, among all available goods and services.

Were it not for the fact that the cost of being governed has risen higher and higher over the years, this would not be an important factor in any study of the cause of rising wages. But the cost has risen sharply.

The present cost of governing ourselves (cost of government) is about thirty-one times as much as it was a century ago, per person, and aside from the effects of inflation on dollar costs. Or if we express it in terms of wages, the cost of governing ourselves a century ago took about three minutes of time out of each hour of work; now it takes nineteen minutes out of each hour of work.

It is noteworthy that the cost of governing ourselves is now a little more than double the entire share of the national product going to those who have saved. It is more than double the total of dividends, interest, rents, and royalties, even in our nation where these are high because of a fabulous accumulation of capital and savings in various forms.

The effect on wages of the rising costs of government is revealed by the accompanying chart. The inroad has become alarming over the last half century. It has taken almost half — 48 per cent, to be exact — of the increased productive capacity of an hour of work over this period. The increased cost of governing ourselves has, in other words, absorbed half the increased welfare which improved production techniques have made possible during the twentieth century.

Government versus Self-Control

Let's put it another way. Suppose it were possible, in some way, to govern ourselves with the same proportion of our working time as prevailed a half century ago. Were this possible, the amount of income remaining to the worker for free choice in his spending — his pay after taxes — presumably could have risen at least twice as much as it has. Our increased capacity to produce, if allowed to operate to the full, could have doubled our increase in economic benefits.

In closing, I would emphatically suggest that perhaps the

70

best way to get higher wages now would be to hire out to ourselves individually, so to speak, for more of the job of governing ourselves. That would mean more self-reliance, more self-control, and all the rest. In this way great savings could be made in the drain on our incomes, leaving that much more to spend on things of our choice and preference. This, in effect, is the same thing as a rise in wages.

Those of us who labor for a living might well consider a completely new direction — a new objective — in our bargaining for wages. Since there is no more to be gotten from employers than the slow increase in productivity will allow, perhaps we should start directing our bargaining power at government. Why not govern ourselves more, and thereby be able to keep more of what we are nominally paid?

A dollar saved is a dollar earned.

9. Losing Pay Through Fringe Benefits

When you can't use your income for things of your choice, its worth is lessened to you.

The greatest opportunity now for a quick increase in the worth of wages is to reduce the cost of governing ourselves so that more of the wage can be kept.

But there is another aspect of free choice in the spending of wages, by which it is possible to raise the worth of wages even further.

The communists-socialists have a plan for society that goes like this: "From each according to his ability, *to each according to his need.*"

This communal blueprint is appealing enough on the surface. Each of us wants to do the best he can according to his ability. And who among us doesn't yearn to have his needs fulfilled? So this slogan sounds like Heaven before the hereafter.

The barb in the bait lies concealed beneath the pleasant dreams of a utopia. For the brutal discipline of reality rules over hopes that can't be hatched.

The catch is twofold. First, as a member of a communist-socialist society you shall not be allowed the privilege of pursuing the release of your abilities at a task which seems best to you. A central authority will decide this for you and for everyone else. He will do this in order to keep a workable ratio between the persons on the stage and in the audience at the opera; in order to have passengers who will ride the trains instead of all being engineers; in order to have someone who will take care of the sewage, and the like. The Commissioner of Opportunities to Work will command you to work at the job of his choice, not yours. You may neither strike nor quit nor change to another job more suited — as you see it — to your abilities.

Needs — in Whose Opinion?

The second catch in this slogan is that your official allotment "according to need" will have no necessary relationship to your hopes and expectations. For it is the central authority, not you, who decides on your needs. And so the Heaven of your dreams turns into a sorrowful reality. Even a child knows this important distinction, such as the difference between the soda he needs and the soda his father proclaims he doesn't need.

Under communism, the central authority decides whether it is bread or cake you "need." If he thinks you need boogie-woogie instead of Beethoven music, or vice versa, that is what you will get. The education he decides you need will be acutely attuned to an understanding of the reason why your welfare is supposed to depend on his staying in power. All these "needs" will be decided with a cold, inhuman arbitrariness. Since the Commissar of the Peoples' Needs never met you — probably doesn't even know you exist — his decisions can't possibly come even close to your version of your needs.

And even though the Commissar chanced to know your wishes, his job is to ration acutely scarce things, labeling them "your needs." Production is low under such a system. And whatever its amount, even with all his power he can't provide for any needs beyond what is produced, less a heavy handling fee.

Under the communist regime there is another side, too, to this matter of providing for your needs. He will also prohibit you from having what he thinks you don't need. This, in fact, becomes a main part of his task under the poverty of communism.

Compulsory or Forbidden

A punster once remarked that life in a communist country means that everything not compulsory is forbidden. And in like manner, the communist-socialist slogan should probably be reworded as follows: "From each according to his ability, and keep from each what he does not need."

Complete and thorough communism has been rare in the world because it is a highly perishable system. Rebellion constantly arises out of the biological, mental, and spiritual nature of man. So the dictator's policies must be "realistic," i.e., they must be moderate enough to enable him to stay in power. A certain amount of freedom of choice must be allowed.

The less-than-complete patterns of communism which exist in various nations go by another name. They have become known as Welfare States.

We need not look afar to some foreign country or ancient society to find this communist policy in operation, in a lesser degree. We have it in our own nation, in widespread forms and instances. Probably each of us is a victim of some of this same type of authoritarian control that we criticize severely when we see it being practiced in Russia or Britain or elsewhere. So perhaps a little soul-searching is in order.

We need especially to review the growing pattern of wage payments which incorporates some of the same idea — "according to need." There is growing up in our midst what might be called corporate welfare states in miniature, or union welfare states. Their effect on the real worth of wages is what will mainly concern us here.

The Total Wage Concept

In order to see the nature of these miniature welfare states in relation to wages, it is first necessary to recall that there is no way to consume this year something to be produced next year or the year after. This remains a simple truth even in an economy like our own where some persons are employed by others and paid with money wages.

Wages have no worth except as one can buy with them something he wants, including the investment of savings. So no matter what the rate of pay or the form of payment, there is no way to pay wages making it possible to have something this year that is not to be produced until next year or the year after.[1]

The simple economic law that wages follow can be seen most clearly in the life of an isolated pioneer. He has what he can produce, and no more. His "wages" are limited by the amount of his production.

What is produced is likewise the "total wage" of an iso-

---

[1] See Chapter 2, p. 14.

lated communal society, or of a nation having a balance in external trade. Production rules the wage limit even in a society otherwise controlled by an iron-fisted communal dictator.

No matter who cuts the economic pie, it can't be cut into pieces which combine to a total that is more than itself. If cut so that one piece is larger, another piece or pieces must be correspondingly smaller. The only way one piece can be enlarged without penalizing the others is by increasing the size of the pie — increasing productivity and total output.

But we are not here discussing such matters. We are, instead, starting with the assumption that this problem of dividing the total of production in a given year has already been resolved satisfactorily for the individuals involved.

Your Share of the Pie

Now let us look at your share of the pie, the part you have produced. It is yours by rights, because you have produced it. And your employer recognizes and accepts it as yours.

He will let you take what you produce in that exact form, if you so desire. But you don't. Perhaps you make castings for trucks; you can't eat them or wear them yourself. Or you may make caskets; you surely don't want them — at least not more than one, and not yet. Or perhaps you teach; what teacher wants to be paid a wage composed of listening to his own teaching?

So you want to be paid the *money equivalent* of what you produce, not what you produce in fact and in kind. You do not want to peddle the products you make, yourself. You want them to be sold by the specialized and efficient sales setup of your employer, which is much to your advantage. Then the sales price, in effect, becomes your wage.

Let us say that last year you produced products of the average amount for a United States family — about $6,000 worth. Taxes took about $2,000, leaving $4,000 net after all types of taxes.[2] This money can be spent by you for whatever you want most.

What you choose to buy is not at all the same as the choices of the man who works next to you in the same plant. This can be seen by comparing notes with him as to what, precisely, each of you did with your last pay checks — every cent, even down to the brand of bread you prefer or where you went on your vacation. If any doubt still remains, compare the choices of hats and dresses your wives bought with some of the money. The techniques of mass production and standardized assembly lines do not carry over into what employees want to buy with their wages.

I Spend It for You

Suppose I take your $4,000 and spend it for you. This means that I shall spend it for what I think you need, not for what you think you need. In other words, I'll probably spend it for the same things I would buy for myself if it were mine, because that is what I am most likely to consider to be your greatest need. I'll have to deduct a sort of commission for my trouble, of course.

What does your $4,000 become worth to you if I handle

---

[2]What you can spend is the net after paying taxes, which last year took about one-third of the pay from each hour of work, in both direct and indirect taxes.

it that way? Remember that I am going to subtract a commission for handling its spending for you; then with what is left, what would you pay for what I select for you? The resulting figure — what you would pay for it — is all that your $4,000 wage would be worth to you under such a plan. That figure can be compared with your $4,000, which you might have taken yourself to spend for your greatest needs as you saw them rather than to give it to me to spend for you.

Assume, for instance, that you say my purchases are worth only $3,000 to you. This would mean that a wage of only $3,000 to be spent by you is as acceptable as $4,000 which I spend for you. There would have been a $1,000 loss, or one-fourth of your $4,000 wage. It means that the real worth of your wage became only $3,000, instead of the nominal figure of $4,000. Your share of the pie — the part due you because of your having produced that much — would have shrunk by one-fourth.

Fringe Benefits

Fringe benefits, as they are called in prevailing jargon, are precisely of this sort. They have been a major objective of union leadership, and have been increasing more and more over the years. The term has even been adopted by employers, journalists, and essentially everyone else. Yet the term "benefit" implies the opposite of the fact, in most such instances.

What, really, are fringe benefits? They are of two types:

One type of "fringe benefit" is the spreading of your pay, which was earned while working, over periods when you do not work. Let us say that you actually work on the job a total of 1,800 hours in a year — an eight-hour day, five days a week, forty-five weeks a year. You might be paid your $4,000 of yearly earnings after taxes in one check at the end of the year; or in forty-fifths at the end of each week you actually work; or some other similar way. Or, if you prefer, the total yearly amount could be paid in twelfths at the end of each month, or in twenty-sixths at the end of each fortnight, or in fifty-seconds at the end of each week — including the weeks and days when you did not work. However it is done, the total will still be $4,000 after taxes.

Some of your earnings may even be paid to you in your old age, after you have retired.

A Costly Convenience

The way you are paid, in this sense, is a benefit to you only as it may be a convenience to receive your $4,000 at certain times rather than at others. It has nothing to do with how much you are paid. It is not a way to get more pay than you have earned — more pay than the worth of what you have produced — so it is not really a benefit, in this sense.

The other type of so-called fringe benefit includes all sorts of things which became substituted for money pay, which you may spend for things of your own choice. Instead of getting your entire $4,000 as a money wage, you may get some of it in the form of specified goods or presumed services. All sorts of things become substituted for money pay. They range all the way from better toilet facilities in the plant to golf courses for members of the families of employees — perhaps even help in building a church of some denomination in the community. It may be more company picnics, or a

Christmas party, or insurance of one sort or another, or a pension for old age — all sorts of things.

Sometimes these "fringe benefits" are the result of employee pressure, either through the union or without any union. But often they are initiated by management; a "company plan" is put into effect.

However they come about, "fringe benefits" of this type have one aspect in common. In each instance its cost comes out of the money due you as pay — out of your $4,000. It reduces the amount left to be paid to you as a cash wage, that you may spend on your greatest need as you see it. It is something that someone else thinks you need.

Fringe Detriments

Most schemes of this sort are not really benefits at all. Employees would be better off, by their standards of need, if they could have the money instead. Then they could buy something worth more to them than any common package, more than any uniform communized "need" that could be devised. Perhaps you don't want any of your $4,000 spent on a golf course because you do not want to play golf. Perhaps you do not want part of your $4,000 used to help build a church of a faith that is not yours. And similarly for other so-called fringe benefits, imposed alike on all employees. You may not want them at all in your current budget, or if you do want them you may not want them under this plan because you may be able to make a better deal elsewhere.

To illustrate, let us say that for every dollar taken out of your income for a "fringe benefit" by someone else's idea of your need, you get something worth only 75 cents to you.

80

Then it would have been worth one-third more to you to have gotten the dollar instead — for a dollar's worth of purchases as you appraise them. For anyone to speak of a loss of 25 cents out of the dollar as a benefit is a strange use of the word, indeed. Rather, it is a *negative fringe benefit*.

My dictionary says that the opposite of a benefit is a detriment. So instead of being a fringe benefit, these kinds of things are really *fringe detriments*. Even then, they are not on the fringe of your welfare; they are as much at the heart of your welfare as any other dollar of your pay.

It is common for these so-called fringe benefits of all types to amount to as much as 10 to 20 per cent of the pay in many corporations now. This amount should be a major item of concern among employees since it is both large and increasing.

Little Welfare States

A friend of mine speaks of them as little, corporate welfare states. And, to be sure, they are just that — if we mean by a welfare state the centrally controlled spending of the people's income for what those in control decide is the need of the people.

A small welfare state is perhaps better than a large one, of course. And it is best to have it where one may move away from its grasp as easily as possible. But an evil small in size and where one can move away from it is still an evil, not a good. It is still of the essence of communism-socialism, wherever and to whatever extent it operates.

So in conclusion, I would say that one way to raise wages is to repeal all these fringe detriments and to set up no new ones; to return full choice, in the spending of the worth of what he has produced, to each individual employee; to give him his wage in the form of money, to be spent on what he most considers to be his need and wherever he can get the best deal.

If several persons want exactly what is offered in the package of fringe detriments, they may still obtain them in the market for goods and services. They may still get the full worth of their incomes in that way, without imposing their desires on all other employees as a "fringe benefit." It is all the others who do not get their dollar's worth. Their income dollar becomes clipped by these fringe detriment schemes, in a manner like the clipping of the coins by the rulers in days of old — for their personal gain.

The worth of wages can in this way be raised at once, anywhere employers and employees decide to do so. It need not await the slow process of increasing productivity. In fact, this is necessary if we are to gain the full benefits possible under our increased capacity to produce.

A Freeze on Opportunity

And as a final point, these schemes of so-called fringe benefits often are a serious threat to our continued progress. Ostensibly their purpose is to reduce turnover of labor and stabilize employment. But they tend to freeze a worker in his job. He does not leave for a more productive job because he would then lose his seniority status and the "accumulated benefits" which he cannot take with him. So he keeps his "security," which the union or the company allows him to have only if he stays where he is. He does not follow opportunity where it leads. "Once a coal miner, always a coal miner," is its effect. This sort of freezing tends back toward the old European caste system, and could bring an end to the traditional American growth of welfare and increasing wages.

So "fringe benefits," rather than coming from pie in the sky, come out of wages — out of what could be paid as money wages. And furthermore, they comprise a serious threat to our progress.

10. Leisure And The Better Life

In the previous chapter two types of so-called fringe benefits were discussed — taking some of one's pay to buy things he may not want, and paying him when he does not work.

One type is not a benefit at all for most wage earners; it is a detriment instead. Part of one's pay is taken to buy something he does not want at the price. Under a centrally controlled plan, which follows the communist-socialist ideal of "to each according to his need," all employees of one corporation or perhaps all members of one union are forced, by a deduction from their wages, to purchase a certain item whether they want it or not. Their "need" is determined by someone else, not by the wage earner himself. And when the purchase is not his own preference, the worth of his wage is reduced that way.

The other type of so-called fringe benefit does not affect, in this sense, how much one receives in total pay. It affects the time when he receives the pay due him. He may receive it either more or less frequently. He may receive a part of it during periods of idleness, rather than all of it when he is actually working. In the sense of his total wages, this is not a monetary benefit to him; it is at best a convenience.

One benefit we all seem to yearn for is idleness — all we can get of it. But do we, really?

Surely we do not want unlimited inactivity. Even in sleep one is uncomfortable if he cannot move and turn about now and then. If a thoroughly well person is hospitalized and forced to be inactive for a day or two, it is said that he would feel about as ill as one who has had an operation. He quickly absorbs his fill of idleness, and wants to make a break for freedom.

So it is not really inactivity we want, in our yearning for more leisure. It is, instead, our desire to be active at something other than our regular activity. We want to be free of what we are currently obligated to do, in order to do something else for a change.

The truck driver wants leisure to get off the road; perhaps he wants to spend a few quiet days at home. But a telephone operator or a watch repairman yearns for leisure so he can get in a car and spin down the road.

The farmer wants leisure to go to the city. The city dweller wants it to go to the country.

The coal miner wants leisure for a plane trip. The plane pilot wants leisure to avoid one.

A hired ballplayer wants leisure away from the game so as to be able to get back home on his farm. The farmer wants leisure to play ball at the picnic.

What most persons do with their leisure costs them money. Yet they probably are paying for the privilege of doing something that someone else gets paid for doing regularly for his living. Two persons might even pay a vacation expense direct to one another for reversing their regular activities.

Welfare and Leisure

As recently as a hundred years ago in this country, as elsewhere in the world over most of its history, a person had to work hard during most of his waking hours in order to provide himself with the food and protection required to keep alive. A hundred years ago in the United States, for instance, the "work year" was a little over 3,500 hours on the job, out of the total of 8,766 hours in a year. Practically all of great-grandfather's leisure hours were needed for eating and sleeping.

With our present advanced productivity, one could probably maintain himself at the level of bare subsistence with the income from as few as 200 hours of work per year.[1] This would provide an extremely humble existence, to be sure, without many things we have come to think of — falsely — as absolute necessities.

We now work 2,000 hours, or a little less, per year rather than these minimal 200 hours. We do this in order to have many more economic things to enjoy, beyond the level of strict necessity.

Choice of Leisure versus Things

This increased capacity to produce above the starvation level of existence allows people to choose over a wide area between more things and more leisure. This increased productivity gives us the choice of either working more hours and having a multitude of luxuries, or having almost complete leisure at the starvation level, or some mixture of luxury and leisure.

After you have worked 200 hours a year barely to protect yourself against starving, you can afford to wonder what

[1]See Chapter 4, p. 28. Also, see *The Conditions of Economic Progress* by Colin Clark. (London: The Macmillan Company, 1951.)

you will do with the next hour — the 201st hour. Probably you will want to continue to work for better food and other economic things you want to enjoy. This is because you have more desire for these things than for the leisure, at this point.

In the 202nd hour probably you will work for still more things, because leisure still has less appeal to you than more things. This would leave 8,564 other hours in the year that could be devoted to leisure.

Moving on up the scale of working hours, a point is finally reached where more work and more things become less appealing than more leisure. So you begin to take a little more leisure. Eventually a point will be reached when almost all the next hour will go for leisure, because it finally comes to have more appeal than does greater material welfare.

Variations Among Men

Persons differ widely in their choices in this respect, of course. The "lazy" person likes leisure so much that only dire necessity or some sort of threat will cause him to bestir himself for much work, because of his high susceptibility to the lures of leisure. Some persons, on the other hand, have strong fortitude and rigidly discipline themselves to purposeful work. They will keep at their work far beyond the starvation level. A few rare persons may even work as many hours as their ancestors did, though their total economic reward would keep 20 or 50 or 100 persons alive.

These are the pleasant choices we have as a result of our present high productive capacity. They are choices between more total income and more leisure which each person may test on his scale of values.

Our incomes per year could have risen even further than they have up to now. But leisure has been chosen in preference to some of the luxurious living that would have been possible with more hours of work. To observe this is not to criticize the choice, since leisure is — in a sense — a form of wage and should be thought of in this manner.

How Much Leisure Chosen?

There has been a considerable increase in productivity from each hour of work since 1855 (see chart). At that time the average work week was about 70 hours.

If we were still working 70 hours a week with present productivity, the total weekly income would have increased the same as the great increase in hourly productivity. But instead, the work week has declined to about 40 hours.

This means that as compared with a century ago, three-fifths of the benefits from increased productivity have been taken in the form of leisure and only two-fifths in more sumptuous living. This presumably reflects, in a rough way at least, something about people's preferences for leisure versus the luxury of more goods and services.

In the middle of the period around the turn of the century, when productivity was increasing slowly, most of the increase was taken in the form of leisure.

The change is what one might expect. The higher your material living, the more you will probably listen to the appealing call of leisure, taking more and more of your rising wage as the "wage of leisure." Or if you don't take more leisure, having become fixed in your habits of work, your children probably will adjust the family tree to the times.

Unions and Leisure

Most labor union officials claim to have attained the shorter work week for workers in the United States. This is a questionable claim indeed.

Union membership now includes little more than one-fourth of all gainful workers.[2] This one-fourth has little if any direct control over the hours of the other three-fourths. And the 40-hour week is widely accepted outside the unions, as well as inside the unions.

The strength of unions and changes in their membership do not justify these claims of having obtained the short work week (see chart). The greatest movement toward taking more of the increased productive capacity in the form of leisure was in the third of a century prior to 1920. Unions were then unimportant, whether measured by membership or by their power over nonmembers.

Up to the late thirties — except for a couple of years right after World War I — union membership was never more than about 10 per cent of all gainful workers. And before the turn of the century their membership was negligible.

The shorter work week of recent decades, when unions have been most conspicuous, is merely a continuation of the previous trend. All the evidence indicates that a shorter and shorter work week would have happened in the absence of unions, simply because persons have always evidenced a choice of more leisure when they can afford it out of a higher productive capacity. So the shorter work week would have come anyhow, with or without unions.

One cannot know for sure, of course, what the length of the

---

[2]See Chapter 1, p. 9.

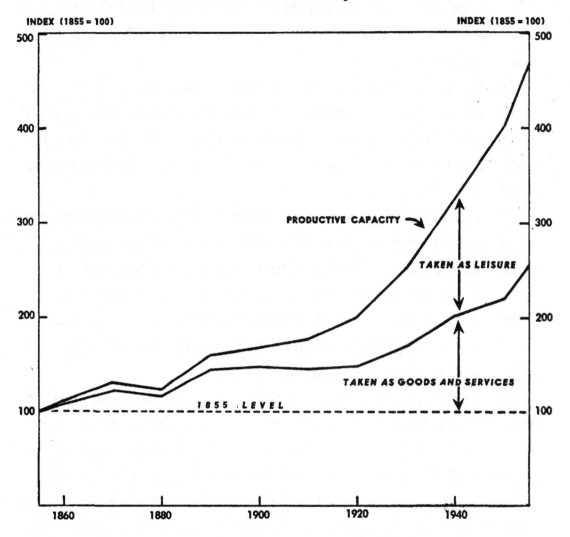

SOURCE: Derived from data on productivity, Chapter 1. *America's Needs and Resources* by J. Frederic Dewhurst, The Twentieth Century Fund, page 695.

work week would now be in the absence of unions. But let us assume that in the absence of unions we would now be working more hours — that unions have, in other words, reduced the work week beyond the free choice of individual workers. If that were the case, the attainment would amount to a disservice to the wage earners. For we would then have to conclude that the workers, under union pressure, have been forced to accept leisure — fewer work hours — instead of their preference for somewhat more hours and increased buying power.

Unionized Unemployment

Unemployment prevails where a person who wants to work for the wage an employer is willing to pay is prohibited from doing so by some outside power. So fewer hours than wage earners would prefer of their own free choice amounts to the same thing as forced unemployment.

Thus, the unions' claim of credit for attaining the short work week is either false or foolish. At best, it is hardly something in which to take pride, so far as its effect on the victims is concerned, because it amounts to having caused partial unemployment every week — *unionized unemployment,* we might call it.

On Vacations with Pay

Among various patterns for leisure, vacations with pay are popular as a supposed benefit to the employee. They are sometimes the object of bargaining by employees, granted reluctantly by the employer. And sometimes they are offered initially by the employer as an act of beneficence.

For the purposes of our concern here, we shall leave aside the question of whether or not a person really needs a vacation — and how long a vacation — from the standpoint of maximum productivity and happiness. We shall assume sufficient leisure for that purpose has already been reached, and that the question now under consideration is an extended vacation beyond this point. Perhaps the employer thought it up as a "fringe benefit" to be given to his employees out of the goodness of his heart, so to speak. So he decides to grant an additional week's vacation at Christmas time, this year and in future years.

Imagine an employer's probable amazement upon receiving from a sharp-thinking employee a note like the following:

> Dear Employer:
>
> I have just noticed on the bulletin board that you are granting us an extra week of vacation at Christmas time, with pay. Thank you for your good intentions. But I sincerely request that you rescind your action. And I'll tell you why.
>
> You and I know that you can't pay us for not working during that week, except by taking from our pay for the other weeks of the year. It has to come out of what we earned in the other weeks of this year. And in coming years it will have to come out of what you could pay us in the other weeks of the year in lieu of this week of vacation.
>
> So when you say it is to be a vacation with pay, you are being misleading. What you must really mean is that it is to be a vacation without pay, but that we will be given some pay in that week for work done earlier in the year and already due us — held back at that earlier time, so as to be available to pay us during this week of vacation.
>
> Or look at it this way: If we were to work that week instead of vacationing, we could produce about 2 per cent more in the year than if we didn't work that week. And if we worked, you could pay us about 2 per cent more for the year than if we didn't work.
>
> So, really, this is a *vacation without pay* rather than a vacation with pay, so far as the year's total pay is concerned.

I for one am sorry you are doing that to us. You no doubt have been overcome by this so-called "spirit of Christmas." But my family needs the extra $75.00 of income more than I need the extra week of leisure. As it is, we have hardly enough to buy Christmas presents for the children anyhow, after paying our taxes and meeting all our other bills. We need the extra $75.00 for Christmas, not a week of unemployment. Then we can help Santa a bit with his gifts for our children at Yuletide.

Please reconsider this fringe detriment — this partial unemployment — you have imposed upon us.

Sincerely yours,

Employee

This type of analysis of vacation benefits will apply equally well to many forms of partial unemployment "with pay." It is clear that there can't be idleness with pay unless there is at some other time an equal amount of work without pay. "Vacations with pay" are an accounting device only. They are really vacations without pay, no matter when and how the pay checks are arranged during the year.

Looking to the Future

If the uptrend in our productive capacity continues as in the past, we shall be able to continue to choose between more leisure and more economic things. How far leisure may eventually go, we have no way of knowing. Automation and atomic power hold untold possibilities of this sort, unless a loss of liberty should terminate progress.

One can see in the future, however, a great and increasing problem of what is to be done during increasing leisure, as we can afford more and more of it. Looking toward a better life and a more peaceful society, we can surely see how leisure may tend to erode both virtue and wisdom. We can surely see the danger of a serious leisure-disease developing among mankind, a disease which work formerly restrained. For work apparently has some sort of therapeutic quality so far as virtue is concerned. And its substitute under leisure seems not yet to have been found.

For instance, in my files is evidence from capable authorities pointing out that the shorter work week is an important cause of crime; how leisure puts many of its victims into penitentiaries where they must be cared for and serviced at a cost to be borne by people who have done no wrong in this instance.

Evidence in my files also indicates how certain authorities assert that compulsory unemployment devices, such as child labor laws coupled with required presence in school buildings during teen-age years, are important causes of juvenile delinquency.

Mental problems of all sorts, too, may in some important degree be the product of increasing leisure.

The paradox of all this is that it may be the problems which leisure brings that will, in the future, offer unlimited opportunities for work in solving them.

So in conclusion, increased productivity has gone more and more into leisure in preference to a more sumptuous life. As a result, yearly wages are not nearly as high as they could be if we had not prized the leisure more, if we had not chosen it instead. But once having made the choice this way, leisure itself creates serious problems which are suggested without being resolved.

11. Pricing An Hour Of Work

The general level of real wages is determined by what is produced. Inflating pay beyond this point raises prices but does not raise the worth of the wage in buying power. Unions, with all their political and other power, cannot veto the iron ceiling that production sets over real wages.

The lone pioneer's desire for some meat, some wheat, or a log cabin is the incentive which drives him to produce. Anticipating his future wants, he produces in advance, like a squirrel which gathers and stores nuts for winter. And in anticipation of years of future use, he makes himself some tools to aid in his labors and in the enjoyment of living.

Then having produced these things, the pioneer is his own sole market. In this situation there is no pricing problem because there is no money and no exchange. Nothing remains unsold as a result of the seller setting his price too high.

Production Creates Own Market

But we are not lone pioneers. We live, instead, in a complex economy. A person usually produces a specialty, selling most of it to many persons and buying his varied needs from many other persons.

Even so, the over-all situation is the same as for the lone pioneer to the extent that no more can be bought than is produced. Despite the fact that some goods and services are exchanged for others, and despite the fact that money may be used to facilitate these exchanges, what is bought still equals what is sold. Just as in one exchange the buying equals the selling because the same item sold by one person is bought by another, so likewise for the total of all trade in a complex economy, all buying equals all selling.

And this leads to the unavoidable conclusion that *production creates its own buying power in a free economy.* Sales equal purchases and purchases equal sales, in total for all trade as for a single trade. Only if the market is not free, only as freedom to trade is interfered with, is this not true.

The Function of a Free Price

The function of a free price is to accomplish in a complex economy of exchanges what the lone pioneer accomplishes in his separate existence — the production of what is wanted of each thing, and no more, insofar as is possible. The function of price is to discourage production of unwanted items and to encourage production of what is wanted, to the extent that wants can be anticipated and production plans can be carried out.

The lone pioneer has his own troubles in this respect, of course. Perhaps the fishing is not as good as he had expected, or the weather not good for the corn. Perhaps in winter he changes his mind about what he wants, wishing he had provided more venison and less corn. Or perhaps his wife wishes the cabin had been fixed up a little, even if it had meant less hunting. Or perhaps too much food was stored and some of it spoiled. What does he do then? He just blames himself for his lack of foresight and adjusts as promptly as possible.

96

In a complex economy, similar events occur. But one person can blame another more easily for not having foreseen the weather, or for the change in his wife's wants, or something of the sort. But the objective of everyone in a complex society should be the same as if he were a lone pioneer — to adjust as promptly as possible and go on with production and living.

That is the task performed by prices that are free. The accompanying chart on the effects of price freedom shows

EFFECTS OF PRICE FREEDOM

If the price is fixed at	these quantities will be		
	wanted	offered	traded
50c	I	IIIII (SURPLUS)	▯
40c	II	IIII (SURPLUS)	▯▯
30c (=free market price)	III	III	▯▯▯
20c	IIII	II (SHORTAGE)	▯▯
10c	IIIII	I (SHORTAGE)	▯

how this takes place, and how an unfree price prevents adjustments in economic living.

The two simple ideas behind this chart are these:

1. Less of a thing will be wanted at a high price than at a low price, progressively.
2. More of a thing will be produced in anticipation of a high price than of a low price, progressively.

From these two rules it can be seen how the quantities available and the quantities wanted operate like the two ends of a seesaw. A rising price pulls down the "wanted" end and pushes up the "offered" end. A falling price pulls down the "offered" end and pushes up the "wanted" end.

Only when the seesaw is on the level, at the point of the free market price, will there be equality between what is wanted and what is offered. And this is the only sort of equality that should ever be given any economic merit. When individuals are left alone, free to buy and to sell what they wish at the price determined solely by the owner-traders of each item, this equality will operate just as water seeks its own level. No superplan is needed to force prices either up or down to this level. Price will find its own level through the innumerable decisions of individual buyers and sellers.

What any outside force does to prices is to push them either above or below this point of equality. The agent who applies the force is always an outsider to the deals of trade, someone who owns neither what is being sold nor what is being traded for it. He is an economic interloper, with or without official title of some sort.

Forcing the price above the equality point creates surpluses. The higher the price is pushed, the greater the surplus. And forcing the price below this point creates shortages — more and more shortages as the price is pushed down more and more.

Two forces operate to create a surplus as prices are forced above the free market point — consumers want less and producers bring out more. And conversely, these two forces both operate to create a shortage as prices are forced downward.

And finally, as to the function of a free price, it will be noted that trading will be greatest at the equality point, a free price. Either above or below that point trading is lessened, either because things are not wanted at a higher price or because they will not be produced and made available at a lower price.

So if we accept the fact that economic welfare is at its best when willing trading is at its greatest, we must also conclude that economic welfare is greater at the free market price than at any other point. If prices are forced away from the point of the free price in either direction, that destroys economic welfare.

Wages Are a Price

The purpose of discussing the function of price in this detail is because a wage is a price, too. It is the price of doing work, just as the price of a bushel of wheat is the price for that embodiment of economic service. In both instances the owner — in one case the owner of the wheat and in the other case the owner of his own time and effort — is entering the market with something to sell. And buyers who want either the wheat or the work enter the market to buy and thus satisfy their respective wants.

The laborer as a person is not a commodity in either instance, but the time of one and the product of the labors of the other are items of sale — both in a like sense.

A worker may work for himself producing some product he sells on the market. Or he may sell his productive services to another person, who in turn sells the product on the market. Or he may work at some task like that of a household servant.

Since wages are a price, they are subject to all the rules of prices and pricing, the same as anything else. All that has been said about the function of price applies to wages the same as to wheat. There is a point of equality at the free market price where the supply of labor and the demand for labor find a balance. And there is no other point of wage-price where this is true.

As wages are forced either above or below the free market point, there will be created either a surplus or a shortage of labor. And there will be less employment either above or below the free wage point — less labor traded — to the extent that higher wages discourage those who might want to employ help, whereas lower wages discourage people from wanting available jobs. In one direction from the free price, employers offer fewer and fewer jobs; in the other direction, fewer and fewer persons want jobs.

Bargaining for a Wage

Bargaining over wages should have no other purpose, in terms of economic welfare, than to find the free market price for the labor involved. For that is the only price of labor where there is economic equality. It is the only price of labor where employment will be at a maximum.

How can one know whether the free market price has been found? So far as I can see, this can be judged for sure only after the fact, on the basis of the consequences. Let us first look at the pricing of some other product.

Suppose you are taking your sweet corn to a consumer market to be sold. You guess where the price should be set for it, and start selling at that price. If at the end of the market day you have some corn left unsold, you will know it was priced too high. And if you could have sold more at the price you set, you know that it was priced too low. How else could you know for sure where the right price was? Note that this has nothing whatever to do, precisely, with what your wife — the bookkeeper — said it had cost you to produce the corn — a figure that might be above or below the free market price.

It is the same with selling your labor. If other employers want you at the price you are getting, or perhaps more, your price on your services is too low. If, on the other hand, nobody wants you at the price you ask, your price is too high. And here as with the price of sweet corn, this figure of a free-price wage for yourself has nothing to do with the cost of producing you; it doesn't even have anything to do with your cost of living, which you adjust to your income rather than vice versa.

Unemployment

When wheat is priced above the free market level, the accumulation that is unsaleable at that price is called a *surplus*. When the comparable situation arises among the working force of a nation, we call it *unemployment*. This refers to the labor — perfectly good labor — which is going unsold at the wage-price.

I would define unemployment as *involuntary leisure of a person who is willing to work at the free market price.*

The only way there can ever really be a surplus of labor, unwanted at the price, is by some sort of force being used on wages to keep them above the free market price. It couldn't happen otherwise. For it seems fair to say that if I don't want to work at the best price the highest bidder for my services is willing to offer me, I am merely preferring idleness to work. And if I thus prefer idleness to work, I am not really an unemployed person. My situation is best described by saying that employment is just not an object of my yearning, sufficient for me to merit the use of the label "unemployed."

A Willing Worker

To illustrate differing ideas about this problem of unemployment, let me cite one incident. The French scholar Bertrand de Jouvenel once told me of his coming to the United States for the first time in the early thirties. He had heard of the tremendous unemployment here, and was greatly concerned about his future, for when he landed in New York he had only eleven cents in his pocket. Yet he quickly found work, in a land where about one-third of the "gainfully employed" of this country were at that time "unemployed." He took a job washing dishes in a restaurant at the wage being offered. He considered the United States in the early thirties to be a land of opportunity.

Jouvenel would probably say, with some justification, that if I were to decline to work at the free market level of

102

wages — whether under the pressure of my government, as in the thirties, or under the pressure of the labor union — I should more accurately be described as suffering from power-enforced leisure rather than unemployment. For voluntary lack of work is not involuntary leisure — not unemployment as I have defined it.

Despite this, however, we shall be using the term unemployment hereafter in the conventional sense, to refer to persons among the normal labor force who are not, at the time, working.

The Demand for Labor

The demand for labor is not a fixed thing. There is not an unchanging number of persons wanted for work. The number demanded depends on the wage. I do not, for instance, happen to employ even one person around my residential property. The price of labor available there is too high for my need of work to be done. But at a lower price for doing work, I would hire one person; at a still lower price, perhaps two persons; then three; and so forth.

Some commodities have a type of demand which we call "unity," where one per cent more of the commodity is wanted after the price is lowered by one per cent. And vice versa.

Apparently the demand for labor is not of this one-to-one ratio. Two noted students of this subject who have studied it carefully — Douglas in the United States and Pigou in Britain — both arrived at similar results.[1] A consensus of their

[1]Douglas, Paul H. *The Theory of Wages.* New York: The Macmillan Company, 1934. p. 501.

Pigou, A. C. *Theory of Unemployment.* New York: The Macmillan Company, 1933. p. 97.

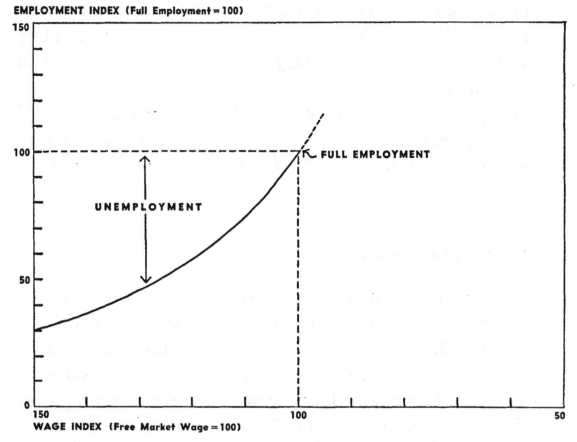

conclusions puts the demand for labor at something like three or four to one. That is, a decline of one per cent in wages would uncover new jobs for 3 or 4 per cent more work. And vice versa.

This idea is of tremendous importance to economic welfare, especially under conditions which threaten a depression. I do not know for sure that this 3 or 4 per cent is the correct figure. But whatever the exact figure, it works in the same way. The difference is only in the rate of response, in new jobs available at differing wages.

Let us take these Douglas-Pigou figures, leaning a bit on the conservative side of their conclusions. Let us say that the figure is 3 per cent. What would this mean when applied to real life?

The accompanying chart of the wage level and unemployment shows how unemployment and the wage level are related on this three-to-one basis.

At the free market wage of 100 (base scale) there is full employment — no unemployment. Everyone who really wants to work has a job.

Now assume that wages are to be forced above the free market level (moving leftward from 100, on the base scale). Employment declines — unemployment increases — at a rapid rate, according to the factor of three. Starting from whatever level one wants to consider, a one per cent rise in wages will reduce employment by 3 per cent.

Wages about 10 per cent above the free market price would mean unemployment of about one-fourth of the working force.

If wages were to go up about 26 per cent, it would unemploy about half the working force.

Too High a Price

How can we tell whether the price of work at a given time is too high? All we have to do is to look at the unemployment figures, assuming the figures to be accurate. Or one might ask people who are not working whether they have turned down jobs at the price offered, or whether they are out of work because they couldn't find any jobs at any price.

Moving in the opposite direction of wages below the free market price (rightward from 100, on the base scale) results in the opposite tendency. More and more people are wanted for work. But since there is full employment at the free market wage, reductions in wages from that point can cause "negative unemployment" only under special conditions. New persons not normally in the working force may be pulled into jobs at a wage below the free market point if they can be induced to do so under the urgency of war, or something like that.

Overfull employment seldom happens except in wartime, for two reasons. One reason is that wages tend quickly to bounce upward to the free market point, there being no potent and effective force in the nation to hold them below that point for long. This is because wage earners are voters, and they do not form unions to keep wages below the free market point.

The other reason why "negative unemployment" does not last long is that the labor statisticians soon conclude that their count of the working force must have been wrong before. So they revise their figures in such a way that full employment is not exceeded, according to the newly revised statistics.

Such is the problem of pricing work in the market for labor. Such is the function of freedom in wages.

12. Riding The Waves Of Business

In pricing one's work, wages are subject to all the influences and characteristics that affect any other price.

Price has an important function to perform. It equates the wanting of things with the supplying of things. The two are in balance only at the free market price. Any other price, either higher or lower, causes a surplus or a shortage; it reduces trade; it penalizes economic welfare. And in like manner, if the price of work is too high, it causes a surplus of labor — "unemployment."

A Powerful Force

When one first thinks about the price for work as having a three-times power over employment, it may seem hard to believe.

Looking at only one job, it would seem to be filled or not filled completely. So what does it mean to say that a raise in the wage rate by one per cent causes a 3 per cent layoff of workers? But for the country as a whole it works out that way. New jobs of all sorts are found when wages go down. But when wages go up beyond the free market point, some jobs close down completely and others close down part of the time.

To see how this works, one must look at an entire economy like a nation and not to one little spot like only one job. He must look at the entire market of jobs available at the different prices.

That is what students of the subject like Douglas and Pigou have done for us in their studies. Both of these authorities found that each one per cent higher wage, from the point of a free market wage, will dis-employ 3 per cent or more of the workers.[1]

Wages and Total Income

Even a child knows that the higher his wage the more will be his income — except that it isn't so. This would be true only if one could keep his job at the higher wage. If it were true that I could keep my job anyway, then an infinite wage would seem to be the ideal. The trouble is, however, that jobs are lost three times as fast as wages are raised.

This being true, the highest income is to be found at full employment.

Let us now assume that I change my wage and take the changing employment at my own job. As I raise wages above the free market point, I do not lose my job completely; but I will have to take my share of the loss of work that comes from an excessive wage. As my wage goes up, my job will have to be shortened more and more, by the proportion Douglas and Pigou found to apply.

If we assume that I work 1,800 hours in a year at $2.00 an hour, this is the way my income would work out:

---

[1]Technically, this is an elasticity of demand for labor of −3.0, or a little more.

108

Wage rate	Approximate hours of work	Yearly income
$2.00 (The free market wage)	1,800	$3,600
2.20	1,350	2,970
2.40	1,044	2,506
2.60	828	2,153
2.80	666	1,865
3.00	540	1,620

So my income for the year declines as wages rise above the free market point, for the simple reason that the work I lose more than offsets the gain in rate per hour. For instance, in the rise from $2.00 to $2.20 there is a loss of 450 hours of work at $2.00 ($900 loss); this exceeds the gain of 20 cents an hour on the 1,350 hours ($270 gain). So the net loss is $630 for the year.

Experience with Unemployment

How has this idea worked out in actual experience?

One cannot know the actual free market wage for a nation, of course. There are innumerable jobs and innumerable skills. There is really a free market wage for each person, and therefore millions of free market wage rates for different persons and different jobs.

Perhaps the best way to see how wage rates compare with the free market rate is to measure the surplus of labor unsold in the labor market. In other words, despite all the faults in such a statistic and all the perplexing problems of arriving at a figure, the number of persons unemployed is probably the best reflection of excessive wage rates.

During the first three decades of this century, unemployment seldom was more than a few per cent of the numbers at work (see chart). It was usually no more than those persons moving from job to job, or temporarily out of work for

UNEMPLOYMENT
As a Percentage of Employed Persons

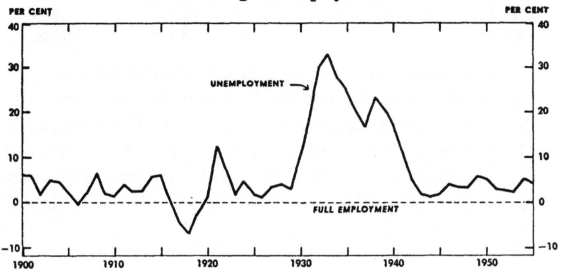

SHARES OF NATIONAL INCOME

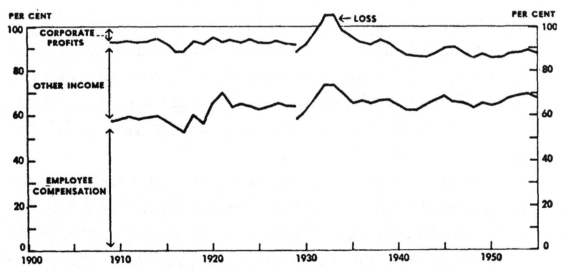

SOURCE: United States Department of Commerce; *The Economic Almanac* of the National Industrial Conference Board; *Economic Report of the President*, January 1956.

The earlier series was discontinued in 1929, and replaced with the new series of the *National Income Supplement, Survey of Current Business.*

some reason other than lack of an available job. The year 1920 was one clear exception, at the time of the postwar collapse in prices. Nor has there been more than the so-called normal unemployment during the years since World War II. In both these periods, then, wages were apparently in line with the free market almost constantly. If they got out of line, adjustment was so rapid that unemployment never became a sustained problem to any extent or for long.

From 1930 to 1941, on the other hand, unemployment rose to a tremendous height — to as much as one-third of the number employed, at the peak in 1933. This indicates that there was a serious overpricing of wage rates during the 1930's.

Wages need not be far out of line on a percentage basis to cause even that degree of unemployment, however. On the basis of the three-to-one leverage, for instance, a wage rate only about 10 per cent too high could have caused that much unemployment.

The Danger of Controlled Wages

It is clear from this evidence that the conclusions of Douglas and Pigou as to the elasticity of wages found confirmation in the tragic experience of the 1930's. It also shows that those who play with wage rates at the bargaining tables are toying with dynamite, not only as it endangers the worker's job but also his yearly income.

It is clear, too, that those who play politically with wage controls are also playing with dynamite. The bitter experience of the thirties illustrates their chronic tendency to play their hand upside down, to the disadvantage of the presumed beneficiaries. Believing that nobody could want their income reduced, they use their power to the full to prevent wage rates from dropping. And the "buying power" theory comes to their assistance at such times, by which it is argued that incomes must be kept up if consumers are to be enabled to buy back the things they have produced.

But keeping income up is not the same as keeping wages up, as we have seen. Incomes move down as wages move up from the free market point.

Why Depressions Disrupt

What happens, then, under conditions like those of the early thirties? At the outset, for reasons we shall bypass here by merely saying that the trouble begins with "monetary causes," the money supply starts to shrink. This causes prices to decline, because less money leads to less price. If absolutely every form of price were to drop by the same amount, no serious harm would be done. Everything would then retain the same relationship as before to everything else, and business would go on about as usual except for the task of changing price tags on things, and such as that.

But prices do not all decline by the same amount. Our concern here is with wages, which fail to drop along with other things. Since they comprise three-fourths of total personal incomes, the serious effect of excessive wages becomes extremely great on the economy as a whole.

Wages are to a considerable extent under future contract. Even without a contract, wage reductions are resisted strongly, even though with lower prices the lower wage would buy as much as before.

112

A wage that is supported at its former level when other prices are declining is the same as a wage increase when other prices are remaining the same. And so in a depression like that of the thirties, supporting wages at their old level puts them above the free market level, just as if they had been pushed upward arbitrarily when prices were stable. The result is unemployment — three-to-one unemployment.

Politicians and business executives also arrive on the stage at about this time to lend their "help." They also try to hold wages up. This is precisely the wrong thing to do. It merely makes matters worse, like doing something to maintain the blood pressure of a person with high blood pressure.

All in all, "help" at such times is dangerous. Controlling wages amounts to threatening the life of the patient, who would quickly recover as he always has done in the past when left to resolve his own problems — if he is free to continue to work at the best price a free market will offer him.

Profits and Unemployment

In his surplus value theory, Karl Marx maintained that profits infringed on the welfare of the worker and should be reduced to zero.[2] The conflict between this theory and the truth, as shown by experience, is revealed by the chart on unemployment and shares of the national income.

In two of these years the surplus value objective was attained, so far as corporate profits are concerned. And in those years the number of persons unemployed rose to a third of the number employed. This was a high price to pay for an extra wage rate of 10 per cent — or whatever the

---

[2]See Chapter 3, p. 19.

113

figure was — as an average for those fortunate enough to have work. The price was especially high for those without work.

The agreement between changes in profits and changes in employment is not exact, of course. But the similarity in a general way is clear. It definitely disproves the surplus value theory. Not only is the theory wrong, it is precisely upside down — at least when wage rates are pressing profits toward total disappearance, as in the 1930's.

Sweeps of the Business Cycle

The notion persists that business swings upward and downward with more or less regularity, and that this is inherent or inevitable under private enterprise. It is also believed that these swings have been getting worse as we have proceeded into a complex economy since the industrial revolution.

This latter notion is a favorite argument of persons bent on socializing this nation, especially those of political inclination. They say that as our economy becomes more complex — more integrated, more urbanized, more specialized — more and more of it must pass from personal ownership and control and be brought under the wing of the government. The reasoning sounds impressive, because the increasing complexity of our economy is perplexing to anyone who tries to see it all at once. But is it a fact?

The chart showing instability of business indicates this to be untrue over the history of the nation. But first a word of explanation about the design of the chart.

The base line of zero indicates a point of no deviations of business from the upward trend of increasing output — more

114

INSTABILITY OF BUSINESS
Moving Average of Variants from Trend
(0 = No Deviations from Trend)

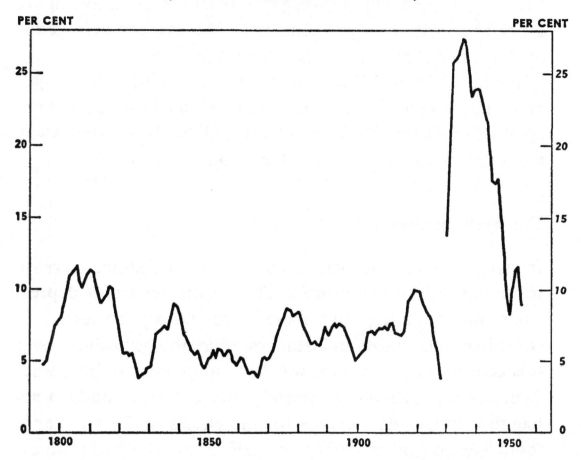

SOURCE: Derived from the monthly figures on business activity, The Cleveland Trust Company.

people and more productivity, over the years. Zero represents unwavering stability, with business running smoothly along the trend of its growth.

The percentages above zero, rising vertically up the scale, represent increasing instability of business. These are the percentages by which business fluctuated around the trend — either above or below the trend, with both considered to be unstable by this measure.

A completely stable business would, then, run along the zero line. At 2 per cent there would be indicated fluctuations in business with a divergence from the trend averaging 2 per cent. And at 4 per cent, twice the average divergence of the 2 per cent point. And on up the scale.

From 1795 to 1928 the average instability was 7 per cent. This means that for the entire period a best guess of the level of business in any month would be 7 per cent away from the trend, either above the trend or below it.

The Myth of Instability

In general, over the period there was no distinct increase in the instability of business. There were recurrent depressions and boomlets, but these were quickly corrected — short-lived, in almost all instances. If anything, business over this century and one-third was becoming more stable rather than less stable; this was certainly true up to the middle nineteenth century. And except for the effects of World War I, there was no evidence of an increasing instability of business even up to the depression of the 1930's.

Then came the Great Depression. A break in the line was made in 1929 because of the violent change in stability before and after that date, making it seem wise to treat the data as two separate series.

Instability of business since 1929, and continuing even up to the present, is something unprecedented in our history. This instability of the last quarter century certainly cannot be called, correctly, a continuation of any long-time upward trend in business fluctuations under our increasing industrialization of the past century. It is something distinct and suddenly new in our economy — a degree of instability above anything we have ever before known in this country.

It is necessary, then, to conclude that the argument about the increasing instability of business is a creation of the imagination or of socialistic invention. Being untrue, it is certainly not a reason for more and more controls over our business affairs. As has been pointed out, controls seem to have done precisely the wrong thing. They have unstabilized business and caused unemployment rather than stabilizing it. It would seem that the controllers know what not to do and put it into practice — rather than what to do at such times.

Business will undoubtedly continue to fluctuate in some degree in the future, controls or no controls. We can expect that. The problem is to adjust as quickly as possible to these changes in conditions, to whatever extent they are beyond our ability to foresee and to prevent.

Cycles Not All Bad

Not all fluctuations in business are undesirable, to be prevented if possible. Take house building, for instance. I have built only one house in my life; and had I continued to live there, I should probably never want to build another. The building of it took about half a year. The result was about as intense fluctuation in my building activity as you could imagine — and intense activity for six months, preceded and followed by building activity at zero so far as I was concerned. I had only one cycle in my building, and then it was all over.

Were a business statistician to study my economic affairs, he would find my house building to be tragically unstable. Suppose he then teamed up with some politician bent on stabilizing business for the general welfare. How would he be able to do it? He would have to determine in advance the probable length of time I would want a house — say fifty years — and then force me to build one-fiftieth of my house in each of those years. That is the only way stability in my house building could be accomplished.

The Human Factor

But being human, I am concerned with my own general welfare, too. As one among supposedly free people exercising economic choices, I don't want to stabilize my house building. There comes a day when I finally decide that I want a house and can afford to build one. I get some help and go ahead with the job as quickly as I can; then it is done. I don't want to be forced to build the house before we want it, and I don't want to be forced to build another one later that I don't want — merely to stabilize some statistic.

And you, I dare say, feel the same about building your house. And so does everyone else.

If as a consequence fewer people want to build houses this year than last year, what is wrong with that? The statistic for the nation is unequal, to be sure, as between the two years. What is to be done about that? Should some people have been prevented last year from building houses that they wanted to build, that they had money saved with which to build, and when building employees and available materials were ready for the job to be done? Or should some persons this year be forced to build houses they do not want, just because the statistic is declining?

This sort of business fluctuation runs all through our daily

118

lives. There is a violent fluctuation, for instance, in the harvest of strawberries at different times during the year. Should we grow enough strawberries in greenhouses so as to stabilize that part of our economy throughout the year?

Sales of toys and Christmas decorations are quite unstable, too. Should we make people buy them equally throughout the year, so as to stabilize production?

Weddings and the sale of affiliated goods and services are highly unstable during the year, and over the years. And so are the sales of baby carriages. Should we stabilize all these month by month and year by year? How?

My own conclusion is that we should not worry about all such fluctuations in business at all. We should worry only about those fluctuations which are due to prohibitions on the rights of each person to work at a job of his choice — either for himself or for an employer who wants his labor — at a wage mutually satisfactory between them. We should worry only about prohibitions on the spending of his income for what he wants most, among things offered by others who have produced them from their own labors.

If we do this, business fluctuations will be reduced to whatever fluctuation people want — not being forced to build houses when they don't want them, or being forced to get married when they don't want to. Wages would then be as high and would rise as rapidly as is possible. Leisure, to the extent one can afford it and wants it, would then be chosen as each person so desires. These conditions would give the maximum of welfare possible for us to attain at any time. It would be as near a utopia as can be hoped for in economic affairs this side of Heaven.

Index